ALL GOD'S CHILDREN?

The National Society

The National Society (Church of England) for Promoting Religious Education is the voluntary body, founded in 1811, which established the first network of schools in England and Wales based on the national Church. It now supports all those involved in Christian education – diocesan education teams, teachers, governors, clergy, students and parents – with the resources of its RE Centres, archives, courses and conferences. The Society publishes a wide range of books, pamphlets and audio-visual items and two magazines, *Crosscurrent* and *Together*. It can give legal and administrative advice for schools and colleges and award grants for Church school building projects.

The Society works in close association with the General Synod Board of Education, and with the Division for Education of the Church in Wales, but greatly values the independent status which enables it to take initiatives in developing new work. The Society has a particular concern for Christian goals and values in education as a whole.

For details of corporate, associate and individual membership of the Society contact: The Promotions Secretary, The National Society, Church House, Great Smith Street, London SW1P 3NZ. Telephone 071-222 1672.

ALL GOD'S CHILDREN?

Children's Evangelism in Crisis

A Report from the General Synod Board of Education and Board of Mission

National Society/Church House Publishing
Church House, Great Smith Street, London SW1P 3NZ

ISBN 0 7151 4808 7

GS 988

Published 1991 for the General Synod Board of Education and Board of Mission jointly by The National Society and Church House Publishing.

Cover photograph by Keith Ellis
Cover design by Bill Bruce

This report has only the authority of the Boards by which it was prepared.

Printed in England by Orphans Press Ltd., Hereford Road, Leominster, Herefordshire.

Contents

The Working Party

Mrs Penny Frank	Trainer Editor, Church Pastoral Aid Society.
The Revd David Gamble	Children's Work Secretary, Methodist Division of Education and Youth.
Mrs Dorothy Jamal	National Children's Officer, General Synod Board of Education.
Mr David Lewis	Children's Evangelist, Scripture Union. Member of the Baptist Church.
Sister Elizabeth McNulty	Area Catechist, Central Area of the Roman Catholic Diocese of Westminster.
Mr Steve Pearce *(until Spring 1990)*	Adviser in Children's Work, Diocese of Southwell.
The Revd Geoff Pearson	Formerly Assistant Home Secretary, General Synod Board for Mission and Unity. Vicar of St Bartholomew's, Roby.
The Revd Gavin Reid	Member of the Board of Mission Decade Advisory Team. Consultant Missioner of the Church Pastoral Aid Society.
Canon Stephen Venner *(Chairman)*	Member of General Synod Board of Education. Vicar of Holy Trinity, Weymouth.

Working Definitions

The terms 'children' and 'evangelism' are frequently used loosely. For the purpose of this report the Working Party defined children as those of 13 years or under. They defined evangelism (in common with the report *The Measure of Mission*) as 'the making known of the gospel of the Lord Jesus Christ', recognising that such a 'making known' requires the creation of formats and contexts in which discovery can take place.

Preface

A Working Party set up between the Board of Mission and the Board of Education is an unusual creature. Both 'sides' approached each other warily. After all, our approaches would be very different. As the Working Party took shape the addition of a Methodist, a Roman Catholic and a Baptist seemed bound to confuse matters further. In the event, the two and a half years of meetings proved to be among the most stimulating I have ever attended. We did not begin from the same standpoint, but our shared and deep concern for children and for the spreading of the Good News led us to a profound and mutually enriching meeting of minds.

It was a privilege for me to be chairman of such a group, and I pay tribute to the contributions made by every member of the Working Party. Our meetings were constantly sparkling with new ideas and insights, so that our only problem was how to sift through the mass of material and produce a document of workable proportions. It is here that particular thanks must be offered to Gavin Reid whose most generous gift of time and talents enabled him to provide the necessary editorial hand on the tiller. Also to Chris Harrison, his long-suffering secretary, who typed innumerable drafts.

The support we received from outside the group was also tremendous. The Mothers' Union membership around the country responded with their customary enthusiasm to our appeal for material, as did many, many parishes and individuals. Some are mentioned by name, others are not. We thank them all. Leslie Francis and David Lankshear, on behalf of the *Children, Young People and the Church* Management Committee, kindly provided the statistical information in the Appendices from the *Children in the Way* database. They were helped by Marjorie Carnelley in the production of Appendix 2. Appendix 1 was first published in *Modern Churchman* in 1991 and is reproduced here with permission. In response to our request, Francis Bridger shared some of his theological expertise with us, and Christopher Lamb gave us some of his thoughts on children of other faiths. The members and officers of the two Boards were generous both in their criticisms and in their support. Members of the

Working Party were particularly grateful for the organisational hard work undertaken by Geoff Pearson during his time at the Board for Mission and Unity, and by Dorothy Jamal of the Board of Education.

We offer this report to the Church and particularly to the local congregations. May they take it and use it to the building up of the Kingdom among All God's Children.

STEPHEN VENNER
Feast of St Boniface, Bishop and Missionary, 1991

Introduction

This report comes as a response to a request from the General Synod made during the debate on the publication of *Children in the Way*[1] – itself a document of great importance.

An amendment was tabled which the Bishop of London, in presenting *Children in the Way,* was happy to accept. The key section of the amendment read as follows:

> this Synod ... notes with concern the low percentage of children presently in touch with the churches and calls upon the relevant Boards of General Synod to give further attention to types of children's evangelism appropriate to this situation.

In response to the passing of this amendment the Board of Education and the Board for Mission and Unity set up a small Working Party drawing in members of other Churches and the voluntary societies. One of the first things the Working Party did was to hold a wide-ranging consultation day with people who had considerable experience of work amongst children. Armed with many ideas, insights (and warnings) the group set about its work and produced this report after nearly two years of reflection.

It was quickly perceived that a practical compendium of good ideas was not what was wanted at this stage. Nor was it felt desirable to attempt a detailed theological or sociological argument. Both such approaches would be assuming a level of interest and motivation for children's evangelism in the churches which the Working Party does not believe to be in place. What the group felt was most needed was a brief, readable document for wide circulation that would alert the churches to the seriousness of the situation, suggest some of the theological and pastoral issues, and indicate considerations that need to be taken in mind as the churches attempt to move forward.

More than anything else, the Working Party members, partly as a result of their research, came to feel that they had a vision and a 'burden' to share with the churches. They decided to write a document that was unashamedly coloured by the sense of urgency they felt after two years of considering their subject.

The Working Party was convinced that children's evangelism should not be judged in terms of instant results and clear evidence of 'bottoms on pews'. It is a Kingdom activity rather than a narrow concern for church recruitment. In working with children whose links with the

1

churches are tenuous, Christians are making a long-term investment in society at large. The Sunday schools and other children's ministry of past decades have given much towards a moral consensus in this country while at the same time accustoming people to the stories and concepts that came alive for many in a later adult commitment. Certainly the evangelistic preaching of the churches has largely relied on hearers having some understanding of the language and thought forms used.

We are now entering a time when we can rely much less on such levels of understanding. If a renewed and numerically effective outreach to children did no more than give rise to future generations of adults who knew what the Church was talking about and who were influenced towards Christian values – that would be a sufficient justification of such an activity.

The members of the Working Party believe that we need a Decade of Evangelism to stimulate us to reach out to the thousands of children who are at present out of contact with the Church's structures. They believe, however, that it would take two to three decades before the full effect of such an outreach would be seen. In this area, and probably in other areas, long-term missionary vision and planning are needed.

It is their prayer that this report will start a major debate throughout the churches and that such a debate will deepen concern and lead to action. There can surely be no more appropriate way to enter the first years of this Decade of Evangelism than to consider how today's children can be brought into contact with the gospel of God and the people of God. This report therefore is a first word rather than an attempt to be a final word. It is deliberately written to provoke thought rather than to prove points. The Working Party recognise that if the challenge of this report is taken up, further research and theological reflection will be required.

We are happy to commend this report for the purpose for which it was written – to stimulate a debate that needs to take place. We welcome this opportunity of co-operation between our two Boards of General Synod. In common with the prayers of the Working Party we sense the urgency of the situation and pray that debate will lead to imaginative and sensitive action. In all this, however, there should surely be no debate about the central conviction of the report – that all God's children need to discover that they are all God's children indeed!

†MICHAEL GUILDFORD   †KEITH LICHFIELD
Chairman   *Chairman*
Board of Education   Board of Mission

1 The Death of a National Custom

But equally there are large groups of people in traditionally 'Christian' countries who belong to the dominant majority community, yet know nothing of Christ. In some countries the old pattern of Sunday school has changed and religious education in schools has borne scant fruit, so that whole generations have grown up without knowledge of the Bible. As societies increasingly become secularised and technology focuses on the material realm, new generations drift into a world where Christianity has limited influence. Many today are unbaptised. This situation calls fro fresh approaches and for a willingness to enter the worlds of others through costly friendships. (*The Truth Shall Make You Free: The Lambeth Conference, 1988* (CHP, 1989) p. 34.)

1.1 Only 14 per cent of children under 15 years of age are in a church-related activity on a typical Sunday. That is one of the findings of the 1989 English Church Census. This report is about the 86 per cent who are staying outside. The Working Party that was set up in 1988 to produce this report made an educated guess that the Churches of all denominations were probably reaching no more than 15 per cent of all children in their pre-teen years. The Census findings proved that this sad guess was all too true.

1.2 It might be argued that a figure of 14 per cent is encouraging in that it is 4 per cent better than the figures for adult church attendance. That, however, would be to ignore two sobering facts. First, that past experience shows that only between 2 – 5 per cent of children attending Sunday school or children's church stayed on into adult church attendance (*Sunday Schools Today,* 1957). Second, that our present adult figures are, at least partly, the fruit of times when Sunday school attendances were considerably higher than they are today.

A NATIONAL CUSTOM

1.3   A survey conducted in 1955 revealed that 83 per cent of adults over 16 claimed to have attended Sunday school or Bible class for several years in their childhood.[1] (A further 11 per cent had attended for a short time and only 6 per cent never.) This would suggest that 50 or so years ago these remarkable figures were the norm. Because of the nature of the sample upon which these findings were based, there is some ground for querying its truly representative nature but even if the figure is severely cut back, it would still suggest that at least two-thirds of the nation's children were in the Sunday schools of one denomination or another in the 1930s and 1940s.

1.4   While it is true that only a disappointingly small percentage stayed on without a break through adolescence into adult membership, the figure suggests that the majority of English adults in the 1950s (and, probably, the 1960s) had some grounding in the Christian faith – albeit at a very elementary level. Further, that grounding came from learning about Christ from the community that believed in him.

1.5   The 1955 survey mentioned also revealed that 54 per cent of English parents claimed that their own children were attending Sunday school. That figure exactly matched Gorer's finding in a 1951 survey. Thus it appears that a downward trend was taking place from the likely figures of the preceding decade. Downward or not, Gorer in 1955 still believed that Sunday school attendance: '… can be considered a national custom; apart from very young parents, the figure only falls under 60 per cent in the metropolis and in the upper middle class'[2].

1.6   We can assume that about half the nation's children had a link with church Sunday schools in the middle 1950s. If true, then about 5 million English children were learning about Christ and his Church and those children are now mature adults in their 40s and 50s with their own children now in adolescence and young adulthood.

SUCCESS OR FAILURE?

1.7   Was the Sunday school of old a success or failure in terms of Christian mission? Two things stand out on the 'plus' side. First, the numbers were impressive. Far more children were 'in church' than adults. Today's figure of about 15 per cent looks pitiful in comparison. Second, with percentage figures of such magnitude it is highly likely that child attendance was drawn from all the social strata of society. The Churches have never been particularly effective in working class districts but there is abundant evidence to show that very many children from working class homes attended. (Indeed the history of the Sunday school movement shows that it began in the late eighteenth century as a more general educational outreach to deprived children.) If any section of society was unreached by the Sunday schools it was more likely to be that nearer the 'top' of the social scale. The founding of the *Crusaders* in 1906 was an attempt to bring the benefits of Sunday schools to the sorts of children whose parents would have felt them socially inappropriate.

1.8   Those who would view the Sunday schools of past generations as a failure can make their point by asking a simple question concerning the high attendance figures. *Where are they now?* As we have already noted, retention levels were abysmal. But the failure of the old Sunday schools needs further examination if we are to avoid making the same mistakes again in some future strategy.

The 'School' model was an inappropriate context for 'learning Christ'. It evolved from historical circumstances rather than theological reasons. The famous Swiss theologian, Emil Brunner, once said: 'The Church took a wrong turning when it substituted the technique of the classroom for the technique of the community in religious education.'[3]

Sunday schools were usually held separately from the normal worship of the congregation. The premises were often at a distance from the church building and the time of meeting was often different. (This had the additional disadvantage that Sunday school teachers were often, themselves, disconnected from the congregation. It was not unusual for a church to have Sunday school teachers who were themselves irregular attenders.)

Because the numerical 'success' was sustained by the national custom of the British way of observing Sunday, the Churches were lulled into a false security. When social changes began to break the mould of the British Sunday, the Churches found they had to compete with counter-attractions and with a change in parental attitudes that had formerly insisted upon children going to Sunday school. The American sociologist Peter Berger has written words that apply here: 'The crucial ... characteristic of the pluralistic situation is that religion can no longer be imposed but must be marketed.'[4] The Churches had no appetite or skill for marketing. Any new strategy that the Churches may wish to launch to reach children today will have to compete for attention.

In a culture where most parents thought Sunday school a good thing to which to *send* their *children,* graduation into adolescence *became a natural point to leave.* One was no longer a child. One could begin to take on the life style of the adult. Adults do not go to Sunday school. It was the other side of the coin of the national custom.

THE DEATH OF THE CUSTOM

1.9   The Sunday school is still alive and well in many places throughout the country. Thousands of children enjoy attendance. Leaders are probably better trained and using better resources than ever before. What they do not have, however, is the benefit of going with a tide of public opinion – the national custom of parentally encouraged child attendance that once gave rise to Sunday school rolls measured in millions rather than thousands. The breakdown of the custom took place in the latter half of the 1950s and the opening years of the following decade. As Britain emerged from the austerities of the Second World War the standard of living began to rise dramatically. More money was available as more options for purchase came on the market. The 1950s began with television sets only belonging to the elite. The decade ended with a set in the majority of homes. Entertainment was privatised at a stroke. All forms of public association began to feel its effects. Cinemas began to close. Football crowds began to shrink. The Churches – while faring better – were affected also.

1.10   Perhaps more significant was the rise in motor car ownership. Increasing numbers of families in all social contexts became proud possessors of a family car. The traditional English Sunday was affected. Instead of a day spent at home centring on a heavy lunch, it became for many a day out in the car. If the parents were not churchgoers it was hard for the children to opt for Sunday school, even if they wanted to. Not only did this seriously affect Sunday school attendance, it also affected Sunday school staffing. Many Sunday school teachers were themselves adolescents, often drawn into teaching as a post-confirmation task. They too came under pressure to drop away when the family custom changed to a day out in the car.

1.11   These new distracting factors came at a time when decline was already happening for other reasons. A Free Church Federal Council report, *Sunday Schools Today* (1957), revealed that declining numbers of children were entering Sunday schools (and that they were only half the strength they had been in 1900). It showed that children who affiliated were leaving steadily through all age groups from seven onwards. It also revealed that only 23 out of every thousand children stayed on into adult membership. There is no reason to believe that Church of England children's work was any better.

1.12   The same survey also revealed the reasons children gave for leaving. Lessons were 'boring' and repetitive and the style and quality of teaching was clearly inadequate. The new medium of television was communicating through pictures rather than spoken words, and a revolution was taking place in the secular classrooms away from 'sit up, look up and shut up'. Further, as children grew older peer pressures came to bear. Going to Sunday school was 'sissy'. The 1944 Education Act with its standardisation of transfer from primary schools to secondary at 11 created a social and psychological graduation point where many children felt they could 'move on' from Sunday school also.

1.13   The effects of the new affluence bringing new life styles, added to these in-built (and too little identified) weaknesses, led to a steep drop in attendance figures in the years between 1955 and 1970. A survey in the diocese of Worcester in 1972/73 noted a 50 per cent drop in Sunday school attenders over the preceding 12 years. It is highly probable that the situation in the Worcester diocese was equally true throughout the country. To put it starkly – in the period 1955-1970 child attendance at 'church' dropped more steeply than adult attendance. While demographic factors probably contributed to the numerical decline, the trend away from church contact was clear and undeniable.

REASSESSING THE SUNDAY SCHOOL

1.14   As the seriousness of the situation hit home, churches (and national bodies) began to respond. Some tried to adjust existing practices. Many churches moved Sunday schools from their traditional afternoon slot to the mornings. There was some sense in this, but it did not address the inbuilt weaknesses of the classroom approach itself.

1.15   Others began to examine the school model more critically. They saw the shortcomings in trying to educate children in the faith apart from the experience of a worshipping congregation. It was also recognised that

7

even if the school model had some legitimacy, the maturity and expertise of the volunteer teachers was seriously defective in all too many instances. Lesson materials (where used) were criticised. Increasingly the theme that emerged was that children ought to learn about Christ in the context of the Christian community at worship.

1.16   Another area that was discussed was the obvious ineffectiveness of the Sunday school as a nursery for future adult church membership. Children simply graduated out in adolescence so as to be more like their parents. Was this not a clear signal that it would be better to try to reach parents *with* their children as a whole family unit? Did this not seem a more 'biblical' way of doing things?

1.17   New strategies of 'Family Church' began to be introduced bringing children and parents together for worship and teaching. The report *Sunday Schools Today* noted that such approaches appeared to hold children longer (seven and a half years instead of six) and led to a doubling of the numbers who carried through to adult church membership (4.8 per cent instead of 2.3 per cent). In the 1960s many churches switched their energies to Family Services with encouraging results. Closer examination, however, revealed that the motivation for this switch was less of a desire to reach children in themselves and more as an evangelistic strategy to reach young parents. There remains a strong case for Family Services but we need to recognise what they are best equipped to achieve. Linked to a positive baptism policy they are ideal as an entrance point into the life of the local church for young parents – particularly those with little familiarity with traditional worship. Viewed as a strategy for reaching the 85 per cent of children at present outside of any church, they have to be seen as ineffective.

1.18   The reassessment of the school model and the development of Family Church raises important issues for all concerned for evangelism. How does one handle a situation where what appears to be theologically more correct turns out in practice to be less effective? It also raises a question to which we will return in Chapter 4, namely, is it right to attempt to reach children in isolation from their parents?

1.19   There can be little doubt that the move away from the classroom to the experience of the Christian community was right theologically. Nor can there be serious argument against attempting to reach whole families as opposed to aiming at children in isolation from their parents. However, the consequences of this richer but narrower approach have to be faced and these consequences are of particular concern for a national Church seeking to minister to the entire community and with a concept of the cure of souls for all within parish boundaries.

WITHDRAWAL FROM THE COMMUNITY

1.20   *The reality of the matter is that a Family Worship strategy reaches little beyond the numbers of children in a parish whose parents are prepared to come.* It has the effect of a withdrawal of influence from the community at large. In the next chapter we shall look at the roles Church schools (and even county schools to some degree) can play in making up for this withdrawal of influence but it needs to be noted that whereas in Sunday school and Family Worship the churches are working on their own territory with those attending 'giving permission' for them to act on their own terms, that can never be the case in a school. *Thus it would now appear that some 85 per cent of the children in this country are growing up without experiencing the gospel of Christ mediated through the community of Christ in a nation which has a Christian Church established by law.*

1.21   At the same time as many churches were moving towards Sunday activities for the whole family, there were also moves towards tighter baptismal policies. Faced with little evidence of child or family attendance at worship following baptism, many clergy and PCCs felt it right to introduce compulsory preparation classes or to require evidence of participation before baptisms could take place. For those who accepted the conditions there was often obvious benefit but the imposing of demands also had the effect of turning some parents (and thus their children) away and added impetus to the decline of children's outreach.

DE-CHRISTIANISING A PEOPLE

1.22   Research conducted in preparation for the report *Children in the Way* revealed that only 393 of the 7,129 churches in the survey had adult congregations of over 200. Of these nearly 52 per cent had contact with fewer than 100 children. Of the 4,186 churches reporting adult congregations of 50 or less, only 1.3 per cent had regular contact with 50 or more children. Researchers David Lankshear and Leslie Francis sum up the matter in stark terms:

> Seven thousand, one hundred and twenty-nine churches provided detailed information about their contact with children, young people and adults on a

typical Sunday. Careful analysis of this information suggests that small churches which contact fewer than 26 adults experience special difficulty in maintaining an effective ministry among children and young people. The seriousness of this finding is assessed against the observation that two out of every five (41 per cent) Anglican churches have contact on a normal Sunday with fewer than 26 adults. (See Appendix 1.)

1.23   One indicator that points to a decline in the churches' outreach to children (or ineffectiveness with those children that they may have reached) can be seen in a private survey carried out by Dr John Mulholland over 24 years among students entering Sheffield University.[5] In 1961 he noted that 94 per cent of students reported 'some religious upbringing'. The figure for 1985 had dropped to 51 per cent. In 1961, 73 per cent claimed to hold some religious belief. This had dropped to 38 per cent by 1985. In 1961, 31 per cent prayed daily. In 1985 the figure had dropped to 9 per cent.

1.24   The outworking of present strategies is that England is nearing the end of a de-Christianising process. As Philip Cliff suggests in *The Rise and Development of the Sunday School Movement*, 'it takes only two generations to de-Christianise a people'.[6] We are now seeing children born to the second generation of non-Sunday school parents. We may have improved our strategy to introduce children to Christ and his Church but vastly fewer children are within our reach. We have rightly been exercised in establishing the proper place for the child in God's Church, but in the process of so doing we have lost contact with the vast majority of the children in God's world.

POSITIVE EFFECTS

1.25   The national custom is no more and the Sunday school which thrived upon it has been found wanting. If it is right for the Church to make a renewed attempt to reach the huge number of children who are not now linked to any of our denominations or independent Churches, we cannot resurrect the past. There are many who feel that any move would be mistaken. They would argue that the Church does not have the resources, and that reaching adults must always be a higher priority. Others would say that the children's evangelism in the past had an innoculating effect that effectively kept Christianity at bay in later years. If only 2-5 per cent were attracted towards continued adherence, how many were put off for life? To counter such arguments it is necessary to look again at the effect of the times when Sunday school was a national custom. Were there any positive results and do they make a case for a renewed attempt to share the gospel with those many children whose parents do not come to church?

1.26 The cross-cultural reach of the Sunday school was remarkable. Children of all social backgrounds encountered Christians and the Christian gospel. Working-class adults revealed that their attitude to Christ was *not* negative. Many of them genuinely wanted their children to be taught about Christ. There was and still remains a deep-seated social and cultural alienation from the churches on the part of many working-class people. At least Sunday school brought the gospel into that culture. Gerald Priestland, in his famous radio series 'Priestland's Progress', coined the term 'the great Church of the unchurched'. He drew attention to the large numbers of people who had a belief in God as seen in Christ, who prayed fairly frequently and believed that they should try to live in a 'Christian' way morally. For many such people joining a church could still be an act of class betrayal or at least irrelevant.

1.27 We need to ask where the faith of those unchurched believers was nurtured. The answer would seem to be – the Sunday school. It is perhaps unsurprising that many observe a change in the content of 'folk religion' over the years. They would claim that it was once basically Christian. It is now (as we shall note in the next chapter) a much vaguer mixture of Christianity, astrology, occultism and fate – a readiness to recognise that there is more to reality than the material, but not much else. The change is something that has developed largely since the death of the national custom of Sunday school attendance.

1.28 While it may be true that over 90 per cent 'graduated' out of organised religion at the end of a period in Sunday school, there is no proof that this was because they were rejecting belief in Christ. The fact was that they attended largely because of the requirements of the national custom and they eventually left *for precisely the same reason*. The requirement was childhood attendance and they had fully met that requirement. There is no way of proving or measuring that leaving Sunday school marked a rejection of Christ, although the body language certainly marked a rejection of Christ's Church. The testimony of many who later in life became church members was not that they had been 'converted' as adults but that they had returned to the faith embraced at a simple level in their childhood years. The low figures for those children who graduated into adult attendance need to be augmented by the considerable numbers of those adults (often on the birth of their own children) who were drawn back into the life of a Christian congregation.

1.29   A survey of nearly 1000 church members (mostly over 35) was carried out by a member of the Working Party. It asked 'How many of you on looking back at the story of your life would now recognise that you took significant steps towards faith before 13 years of age?' The answer came to 65.2 per cent. This would suggest that Sunday school (or other children's ministry) did indeed have an effective evangelising effect in the long term and that present-day church membership is heavily dependent on it. If such a conclusion is claiming too much, it does, at least, demonstrate that children under 13 are particularly open to belief in God. *To deny them the opportunity to learn about him is to deny them something many will value for the rest of their lives.*

1.30   The years since the death of the national custom have seen the break-up of a moral consensus in the nation. Many would point quickly to a decline in standards of sexual behaviour as evidence of this but the break-up is perhaps more significant in the decline of standards of truthfulness, of respect for property or the readiness to keep one's word. It is impossible to prove a connection between the two but it is, at least, reasonable to suggest that such a connection might exist.

1.31   Today with only about 15 per cent of all children under 13 in church-related evangelising activities, the lessons from the past would suggest that the Churches of all denominations are facing significantly leaner times in terms of future membership. The 1989 English Church Census detected a drop in child attendance during the 1980s that was steeper than the drop in adult attendance (although demographic factors may partly explain this). If our present adult attendance benefited from an eventual 'filter-through' from children's ministry in the years when 50 per cent and more of the nation's children were being reached by the churches, how will we fare when the filter-through is from today's much smaller figures?

1.32   There is, however, a more worthy consideration to bear in mind than a slightly selfish concern for Church membership. Can any person touched by the spirit of Christ be complacent about a situation which commits 85 per cent of all young human beings to set out on the journey of life with little or no awareness of a loving heavenly Father and no experience of the Christian story as told and lived out by the Christian community?

2 Any Other Witnesses?

Religious belief, when not associated with active membership of a church, tends to be associated with superstitious belief... (Nicholas Abercrombie, 'Superstition and Religion' in *A Sociological Yearbook of Religion in Britain*, vol. iii, (SCM).)

2.1   If the direct activity of the churches no longer plays any part in making Christ known to the majority of today's children, are there any other witnesses? Is there anything that can soften what appears to be the harsh reality of 85 per cent of children cut off from the gospel?

2.2   In the first chapter the focus was upon the Sunday school and the decline in its influence upon the majority of our children's lives. It would be wrong, however, to claim that the Sunday school was the only source of Christian influence upon children. Before we can conclude that the situation is as serious as the first chapter suggests, we must examine three other sources of influence that may well witness to Christ.

1.   The background influence of 'folk religion' and the nation's Christian heritage.
2.   Uniformed movements.
3.   Church schools.

FOLK RELIGION AND THE NATION'S CHRISTIAN HERITAGE

2.3   While only some ten per cent of English adults are in church on a Sunday, the general population, in contrast with a nation like Sweden, overwhelmingly professes to believe in a God of some sort. Because of the longstanding Christian heritage of the country, the popular concept of God has, in the past, been largely shaped by Christianity. 'Folk religion' is a phenomenon whose existence few would deny. Just what makes up the content of 'folk religion' (and whether the term is appropriate) is more open to debate. Professor David Martin[1] over 20 years ago identified what he called 'subterranean theologies' in England which were totally outside the world of the churches. These were patterns of belief in religious and supernatural matters which were never publicly proclaimed but which were passed on and picked up in the casual conversations of the pub, launderette, bus queue and work place. Any child growing up in England would be likely to encounter such 'theologies'.

2.4 In previous generations these subterranean theologies would have entered a child's awareness mixed with the content of Sunday school teaching. Today this, as we have seen, is significantly less likely to happen. The result of the lessening influence of Sunday school is that folk religion is changing. In a paper related to a Leeds University research project Dr Robert Towler observes:

> ... traditional folk beliefs and folk practices occur ever less frequently, although they show a remarkable degree of persistence. Simple fatalism appears to have a resilience ... Belief in fate as a definite pattern of destiny continues, as does belief in the intervention of good luck in everyday affairs of health, security and employment. Indeed ... while some traditional elements of folk religion fade in importance, others emerge with a new strength and popularity. The discerning of fate by methods of prediction such as horoscopes, the I Ching and palmistry is more popular rather than less, encouraged by the portrayal of these practices in the mass media.[2]

2.5 The Leeds University project, with its detailed survey of the beliefs and attitudes of some 2000 people in the city and its environs, contains elements that are both encouraging and disturbing to those with a heart for Christian mission today. 60 per cent of those interviewed said that religion was either 'very' or 'fairly' important in their lives. 76 per cent claimed to have a religion and 30 per cent claimed to belong to a religious organisation or church. Of the many who had stopped attending or belonging to a church only 5 per cent attributed this to having 'objected to the religious teaching'. The majority, 60 per cent, put their lapse down to the fact that they 'grew up and drifted away'. Such answers hardly reveal a nation that is hostile or philosophically opposed to the Christian faith.

That said, however, the report reveals a disturbing openness (when viewed from the standpoint of orthodox belief) to such factors as fate, luck, the occult, and other forms of superstition. Only 43 per cent believed that Jesus was the Son of God. And only 40 per cent believed in life after death.

2.6 Evangelism (as we shall note in Chapter 4) particularly focuses upon the story of Jesus Christ and the understanding that he is God come among us. While the Leeds survey (in common with other polls and surveys) reveals that the majority of English people are open to belief in God, it also shows that the specifically Christian elements within their 'subterranean theologies' are much less marked. Many of the older people interviewed in the Leeds survey would have had Sunday school experience. The suspicion of the Working Party is that folk religion will become (and is becoming) something which has increasingly less in common with the gospel. There is little here to comfort those who long to see future generations of children encountering a clear and life-shaping faith in their most impressionable years. Rather, the Working Party fears that the observation of social researcher Nicholas Abercrombie may be accurate:

> Religious belief, when not associated with active membership of a church, tends to be associated with superstitious belief ... for those people who do not go to church yet say they are religious and pray often, religious belief has moved quite far from the orthodox church position and is really much closer to what would normally be called superstition ... there is a gulf between orthodox religion on the one hand and superstition and private religion on the other which really makes it impossible to describe the latter as a variant of the former.[3]

2.7 However children may encounter the changing manifestations of folk religion, we must also reckon that they will also encounter reminders of the country's formal Christian tradition. Family events such as weddings, baptisms and funerals are likely to be attended. Acts of worship at school will be experienced. The season of Christmas with its many reminders of the birth of Jesus and great national moments which are marked by Christian religious ceremonies – all these will raise some degree of awareness. It is impossible to generalise about their effects – they will vary from child to child. What must be recognised, however, is that there is very little likelihood of these occasional reminders having any sort of evangelising effect. The mind may take note in a casual manner, the heart and will are unlikely to be engaged. For many children the fact that the Christian religion is referred to as part of the nation's way of doing things could mean no more than noting that in England we drive on the left hand side of the road. The most we can and should hope for is that these reminders nurture an openness and might lead to a questioning mind.

15

UNIFORMED MOVEMENTS

2.8   Thousands of children are members of the various uniformed movements. The Churches have reason to be grateful to the contributions made, over many years, by Scouts, Guides, Boys' Brigade, Girls' Brigade, Campaigners and the Church Lads' and Church Girls' Brigade. Viewed from the standpoint of evangelism, however, a clear distinction has to be made between Scouts and Guides and the other uniformed movements mentioned in this chapter. Scouts and Guides are world-wide organisations serving children of all faiths. As such they are not, and cannot be, committed to Christian evangelism. The Scout Movement, in its fact sheet *Fundamentals of Scouting,* states:

> Scouting is not a religious organisation. The Movement does not align itself with any particular religion. Scouting recognises that there are diverse ways in which God shows himself to mankind.

A spokesperson for the Girl Guides told the Working Party:
> Our movement is not specifically Christian and we are encouraging members of all faiths to join us. However, we are concerned that every individual is given the opportunity to strengthen and deepen their own faith.

2.9   The Cub Scouts have recently introduced a new achievement badge called 'My Faith'. Work for this badge will encourage the child to find out as much as possible 'about being a member of your religious faith'. The child is encouraged to collect photographs, tapes and other items for a presentation and to present evidence that shows an understanding of the life and belief of the faith community. The badge is awarded after consultation between the Cub Scout leader and the priest, minister or equivalent within the religious body. The Girl Guides are shortly to introduce a similar award. Such awards, however, are voluntary and only likely to appeal to those who are already committed to their church to some degree.

2.10   In practice many Guide Companies, Scout Troops, Brownie and Cub Scout Packs have a clear-cut Christian ethos because of their links to churches and the Christian commitment of particular leaders. With a never ending need for volunteer leaders to care for a total English membership of about three-quarters of a million children, these organisations provide a worthwhile and richly rewarding area of service for church members. However, it needs to be recognised that any contribution that is made towards evangelism is likely to be indirect.

2.11   The specifically Christian uniformed movements are much smaller than Scouts and Guides. The total membership of children under 14 in the Boys' and Girls' Brigades, the Church Lads' and Girls' Brigades and Campaigners comes to little more than 94,000. Even if every one of these children were to be counted as an addition to the number of those in specific Church Sunday activities, it would only add one percentage point to the numbers of children being reached by the churches. The reality, however, is that many of the children in uniformed movements are also in the normal Sunday school or similar church activity. (Campaigners, for example, calculate that 62 per cent of their under-thirteens 'attend church or Sunday school'.)

2.12   The great strength and distinctive mark of these movements is that they were founded with an evangelistic vision and, while much depends on the quality of local leadership, that founding vision remains. The Constitution of Campaigners, for instance, contains the following aim:

> The development of a personal faith in Jesus Christ as Saviour and God in the lives of boys and girls and young people...

2.13   These organisations have served the churches faithfully over many years. Their blend of Bible class, club nights, camps and ventures plus the sense of belonging to a national movement have captured the imagination and enthusiasm of many children. One gifted leader of a large church group told the Working Party that he believed the uniform and the structured approach of such movements was a resource that enabled less creative and imaginative leaders to hold children's attention and provide an attractive format.

2.14   There are good grounds for believing that uniformed movements often have an appeal outside of church related families – for example, 64 per cent of those in Campaigners come from non-churchgoing parents. What is true for one of the movements is probably true for the others and this factor needs to be taken seriously. The main complaint which some churches report is that many children in such organisations owe their allegiance so much to the uniformed movement that they do not easily see their local group to be a part of the church.

The same criticism could well apply to other organisations of a local church, not excluding the Mothers' Union. The answer to the problem must surely lie in the close working between clergy and the uniformed movements' leadership and especially in the leadership being drawn from the congregation itself.

2.15 The Working Party believes that church related uniformed movements still have a valuable role to play in introducing children to the gospel. Nevertheless if we are looking to such movements to make up for the dramatic decline in Sunday school attendance, the *present* reality is that their contribution is not significant.

CHURCH SCHOOLS

2.16 In numerical terms, however, Church schools cannot be so lightly dismissed. There are currently 4,936 Church of England schools operating at primary level in England today. Some of these are termed 'Voluntary Controlled' which means that the Local Education Authority is responsible for on-going financial responsibility while the church, usually represented by the Diocesan Education Committee and the Parochial Church Council, retains the right to appoint a minority of the governors and to hold denominational worship. Other Church schools are classed as 'Voluntary Aided'. In such schools the Local Education Authority provides financial aid but the church maintains the main responsibility. As a return, the church appoints most of the governors and provides for denominational teaching as well as worship in the life of the school. In all Church of England schools the parish priest is an ex-officio governor of the school.

2.17 In addition to these figures there are other county schools with no formal church links but where the present realities are that a church–school link in the community deeply affects the school ethos, and where the headteacher and staff welcome and foster the relationship.

2.18 In some parts of the country – especially in rural areas – Church schools form a high percentage of all the schools available. This would appear to present a great opportunity for commending the gospel to children, but there is another side to the coin. Unlike Roman Catholic schools where, until very recently, it was assumed that all children practised their faith, Church of England schools have usually operated a more open policy towards the community at large. In those rural areas where Church schools present the only choice open to parents, many headteachers and governors do not believe they have been 'given permission' to commend Christ in anything like the way that is appropriate in a

Sunday school, Family Service or children's holiday mission. A General Synod resolution in 1985, while asking for the Church's role in controlled schools to be developed to the full, also stressed the twin aims of contributing to the provision of general education in their immediate neighbourhood and at the same time providing a specifically Christian form of education.

2.19 From the point of view of the child in a Church school, there has been no personal choice to consider the story and claims of Jesus Christ. The willingness to consider is an important part of the dynamics of evangelism. In true evangelism we are not coercing people to believe or taking advantage of an inability to escape from exposure to the gospel. In evangelism we are resourcing the search of those who are willing to be open to the gospel itself.

2.20 Church schools vary enormously in their ethos and effects. There is plenty of evidence that many non-churchgoing parents genuinely want their children to go and to learn about Christ. Indeed, there are many parents who look to the school teacher to do two things which they find embarrassing – to teach about sex and to teach about Christ. Clifford Longley of *The Times* once said that the phrase 'a Church of England School' can properly be translated as 'a school where Christianity is taught as true'.[4] There are still many outside the membership of any church who would agree with that definition and welcome it. Conversely, there are also those within the membership of the churches who would have problems with such a definition. They would see the main task of a Church school to be that of providing first class education but doing so within a Christian ethos.

2.21 We must assume, however, that a significant number of children within the 85 per cent who do not come to church learn about Christ through Church schools in a positive way that, at least, makes present or later faith more likely. It is impossible to put a figure to this. It cannot reflect the full number on the school roll because many of the children come from church families and are already to be counted within the 15 per cent figure of those who attend. What we need to emphasise is that Church schools cannot do what only the Christian community can do – give children an experience of the Christian community telling and living out the story of Christ.

2.22 The Working Party hopes that the Church of England will continue to believe in the value of Church schools and that in times when much is in flux in the world of education, parents, teachers and governors will see the value of continuing the strong link between education and the Church. That said, the Working Party did not believe that the present impact of Church schools greatly altered the serious situation affecting children in our country. It is still true that the vast majority of England's children are growing up without learning about Jesus Christ from the lips and lives of those who believe in him.

3 Who is Shaping our Children's Lives?

The world of our children is virtually controlled by the media – which portrays a more exciting world than the real one. Everything is highly coloured, fast, slick, more professional and sophisticated, so that family, home and school can seem boring by contrast. (Pat Wynne Jones, *Children Under Pressure* (Triangle, 1987), p. 93.)

Most of the stories, told to most of the children ... are not told by the parents, not by the schools, not by the Church, but by a small group of distant corporations. (Professor George Gerbner, cited in *The Future of Christian Broadcasting in Europe* (McCrimmons, 1990), p. 17.)

3.1 If Christianity is making so little impact upon the lives of the vast majority of today's children, what is? Where should we look to find sources of influence that might shape those millions of young lives? Two obvious answers are the home and the school.

HOME AND SCHOOL

3.2 Home life for most children should surely be a more enjoyable and fulfilling experience than it was for the children of 100 or even 75 years ago. The standard of living is higher. Children have more options and possibilities. While it is true that unemployment brings a shadow over too many families, and marriage breakdown imposes strains and sadness, it is still the case that some 87 per cent of all children live in two-parent families.

3.3 This said, three things need to be recognised.

1. The effects of the high cost of living on family life.
2. The inability of parents to control the experiential environment of their children.
3. The acknowledged inability of most parents to teach their children about Christ.

3.4   The high cost of living (added to high expectations) means that for many parents debt can be a powerful factor in their lives. For some years home loans have been calculated off a base of two salaries and house prices have been affected accordingly. At one social level the word 'debt' is often used. At another the term 'credit' is preferred. The reality is the same – there is a pressure upon both parents to earn. In addition to these personal financial pressures it is now recognised that the demographic balance of British society means that an increasing number of mothers will be targeted by employers in the latter years of the decade. A previous Secretary of State for Employment has said:

> We are about to experience the most dramatic decline in numbers of new entrants ever known. Between now and 1994, the number of young people leaving school and college will fall by 30 per cent. The traditional source of new recruits will be seriously depleted. [1]

3.5   Quite apart from the pressures on mothers to return to work there is, increasingly, the *desire* of many mothers to return to work and to the furtherance of a career. The 1991 edition of *Social Trends* reported that 40 per cent of mothers of pre-school children now go out to work – an increase of 13 per cent on the figure for 1985. Today's expectant mothers are more likely to talk in terms of 'maternity leave' rather than 'giving up work to start a family'. We are now a society that increasingly needs child-minders and other forms of pre-school care. The amount of time which parents can spend with their children – especially during school holidays – is inevitably affected. *Responsible parents will regard weekends as quality time for the family and for such good reasons are hardly likely to warm towards local church children's activities on a Sunday.*

3.6   The pressures to earn that are upon parents, plus the nature of television, added to peer group influences at school and in the neighbourhood together exert a very significant influence on the parent/child relationship. Parents now cannot control the experiential environment of their children. From educational psychologists we know that the experiences of infants and children have profound life-shaping effects. In pre-television times with the mother remaining at home there was a strong possibility that – if desired – parents could largely control the experiences of their growing children. The phrase 'not in front of the children' reveals an awareness of the importance of protecting one's offspring from experiences that could cause them anxiety.

3.7   In the Old Testament we read that Eli was held responsible and came under judgement for the behaviour of his grown-up sons (1 Sam. 3). It is a judgement that seems harsh to modern ears. It is a judgement that would be totally unfair of any parent today. Television is almost impossible to control. Young children can easily push buttons when parents do not want them to and even successfully operate video recorders. In an article in *The Independent on Sunday* (17/3/91) Maureen Freely writes of an episode in her own home:

> I didn't plan to traumatise my four-year-old by letting him see *Aliens*. But I was busy with a new baby and didn't know there was a copy of the offending video in the house. When I realised my mistake and sat down to watch it I was horrified.
>
> What had I done to my child? Answer: I had turned him into a nervous wreck. For the next few years, Matthew believed there were aliens in the radiators, aliens in the cupboard, aliens gestating under his bed and waiting to burst out of his chest...

Not only is the output of the television set almost uncontrollable, there is the influence of others in the peer group at school – often with their minds full of commercially resourced hype for the latest toy, pop singers, designer clothes and so on. So strong can be the influence of the peer group that parents feel alienated from their children – even before the 'difficult years' of adolescence.

3.8   This does not mean, however, that parents as a whole are fighting a losing battle. Most children in England are fortunate to have caring and responsible parents. The point is that such parents are probably facing a more difficult task than their own parents encountered. Equally important from the point of view of this report is the fact that few parents today would consider themselves competent (or particularly motivated) to teach their children about Christ. That is something they would leave to the school or to a church related activity 'if the children wanted to go'. Their children, therefore, have to be self-motivated or nothing will happen.

It is not uncommon to hear parents say, 'I'm not going to influence my children. It is better to leave them to make up their own minds on these matters.' The flaw within this position is that a stance of neutrality is in itself going to influence the children.

THE ROLE OF THE SCHOOL

3.9 We have already considered the contribution made by Church schools (para. 2.16) and noted the twin aims of providing a general education in the neighbourhood (sometimes with added complications where other faith communities are present in strength) and providing a specifically Christian form of education. What about the county schools? What influence do they have? Do they shape the lives of our children and do they make up for any of the ground lost by the churches?

3.10 Children spend a significant proportion of their time in school. The influence of their teachers, the content of the lessons, the ethos of the school and their relation to (or exclusion from) the peer groups must play a major part in shaping their attitudes to life. Schools and teachers have been experiencing a lack of affirmation in recent years. The Working Party felt that they deserved more than a few bouquets:

1. The interest in and concern for individual children shown by teachers and headteachers is often outstanding.
2. Schools often offer a more stable environment to particular children than their own homes. There were cases known to the Working Party where children from a divided family only met when in school.
3. It is important to note that for very many children (perhaps the majority?) the county school is the only setting where they experience prayer, hear Bible stories and take part in the celebration of such festivals as Harvest and Christmas.

3.11 Two things need to be recognised, however.

The county school (and, in the Working Party's judgement the Church school also) cannot be expected to make up for the decline in the influence of the churches since the death of the national custom of Sunday school attendance. *A school within the State education system cannot be a community committed to the truth of the gospel in the sense that a local church-based children's activity would be.* Thus Christianity is not handled in the same way as science or geography in terms of 'facticity'. The Resurrection is not treated as an unchallenged historical event such as the Battle of Hastings. Children who go through the experience and processes of the classroom will note and be influenced by the difference of approach.

No school is outside our contemporary culture, and all teaching within the school will be affected by the 'reigning tradition' of the culture.

Bishop Lesslie Newbigin describes our current 'cosmopolitan culture' as one where we divide everything into 'facts' and 'beliefs'. 'Facts' – like one and one are two – are universally true. 'Beliefs' deal with such areas as religion and value systems and as such they are *not* seen as being universally true according to our 'reigning tradition'. Thus the Battle of Hastings is seen as a 'fact' but the Resurrection is a 'belief' and belongs to the realm of private opinions. To claim that a matter of faith is universally true runs against the reigning tradition in our culture. It is here that there is a direct clash with a mind that is shaped by the Gospel. For the Christian any 'reigning tradition' in a culture needs to be judged by the life, death and resurrection of Christ – not the other way around. Fact as well as faith is involved when we speak of Jesus. [2]

The second reminder is that teachers and the curriculum are not the only opinion-formers or character-shapers in school. Few influences are more powerful upon growing children than the opinions of their peers. In many secondary schools peer group pressure has become significantly more powerful than any other. This is less true for the age group under consideration in this report (under 14) but it is still a force to be reckoned with. If going to Sunday school or any church related event is considered 'sissy' or 'odd' then the matter is closed as far as many children are concerned. It is not uncommon for parents to be horrified by the behaviour of their children which has been learned from others met at school. We shall return to this factor later.

3.12　We now have to ask – what other potentially character shaping and opinion forming influences are brought to bear upon children today? In what follows, the Working Party believes it is important to set out as strongly as possible what it saw. Our prevailing culture is pluralistic which encourages a 'live and let live' philosophy. This has many positive advantages. It carries, however, the tendency at times not to take seriously matters that should indeed be taken very seriously. In considering the experiential environment outside of school and home the Working Party believes we are in an area that is not being examined critically enough. Who or what, then, is shaping (or even 'converting') our children today?

OUTSIDE INFLUENCES – TELEVISION

3.13　Television enters the experience of children very early in life. In many homes it is the electronic baby-sitter. According to one estimate[3] the average household watches TV for 35 hours every week. Many children have their own TV set (sometimes with video recorder) in their bedroom.

3.14 There are many positive values that stem from this:

1. TV widens the horizons. Children are more aware of being citizens of the world.
2. Knowledge and understanding are improved. TV is genuinely educational.
3. Sport is promoted. Many are encouraged to take up outdoor sport and recreation from seeing it on TV. (Nick Faldo took up golf after seeing Jack Nicklaus winning a major tournament on television!)
4. Television presentations encourage compassion and giving to worthy causes. It is used effectively for this in *Blue Peter*, *Comic Relief* and the annual children's causes *Telethon*.

3.15 It was Marshall McLuhan who suggested 25 years ago that the medium was always more significant than any message it conveyed. Indeed, he argued, 'the medium *is* the message'. This judgement has some strength when applied to television, because the effects of the medium – *how* it communicates and its total diet of programmes – are far more significant as an influence on children than any items particularly designed for them. Further, television is but one of several components in our culture *which have the effect of throwing children, too soon, into the ambiguous world of adult values and activities.* For all the attempts to restrict particularly 'adult' programmes to later hours in the day, laissez-faire attitudes to bedtime plus the video recorder make nonsense of such regulation.

3.16 There are some who argue that the general lack of involvement in passively watching a television set inhibits children's natural creativity at a stage in life when it is meant to be developed, and this may well add to a reduced readiness in later life to face challenge and adventure. 'All the world's a set and all the men and women merely spectators.'

3.17 Television, because it is visual, has difficulty in portraying those realities that are *not* visual. God is such a reality. It has been noted that TV is more convincing in portraying broken relationships than harmonious ones (*Dallas* would have been even more uncompelling if it was full of people constantly being nice to each other). Sir Robin Day, a product of and brilliant communicator within the medium, has some sobering words to say:

> With its appetite for visual sensation, its tabloid dependence on pictures, television had an inherent tendency to distort and to trivialise. Disaster, violence, disruption, were the staple of TV's diet. Television's appetite for them was insatiable. This appetite, this lust for visible action and violent happenings, is itself an invitation to create more of the same for TV to project.[4]

3.18 Because of the medium's continuous requirement for movement and even violence, it presents a distorted picture of reality. Stillness and peacefulness are 'bad television' so little attempt is made to convey such qualities. The child who frequently watches television tunes into a hyperactive world – and further, a world that is slickly presented. Small wonder that he frequently uses the word 'boring' to describe the world that takes place away from the small screen. 'Real' life, however, includes those times which are boring – and there is no remote-control button to punch in search of something more exciting. Unlike the soaps, life has times when marriages are neither deliriously happy nor on the verge of collapse. Further, real life is often about living with unsolved problems and there are few instant solutions.

In the task of communication, Church and school find themselves in competition with the slick, highly financed methods of the TV studio.

3.19 Apart from the general effects of the medium itself there are obvious areas of concern relating to elements which frequently occur within programmes.

3.20 One such area is the depiction of sexual activity. Pat Wynne Jones in her book *Children under Pressure* asks the question: 'How can we teach our children Christian values in a society which has rejected its moral roots ... and where young minds are assaulted from all sides by images and ideas malign to biblical principles?' The problem, however, is more complex than whether children see 'sinful' images. It is whether children are being exposed to certain images (in this case with regard to sex) *before they are emotionally able to cope with them*. Again, we need to remember that television is not the only source of these adult images. Newspapers, magazines and the lyrics of many pop songs can all expose a child to sex and his or her own sexuality long before the age of puberty. A recent magazine for home computer owners contains material that belongs to the world of soft porn. Readership is defined as from 11-18 but with the current enthusiasm for computer literacy, sibling interest must produce quite a few readers at the lower end of the age range.

3.21   Another area of concern centres on the portrayal of violence. We have already seen that the medium almost requires violent images to hold interest. The problem that many have identified in the cinema and on TV in recent years is that violence is no longer the trade of villains. The heroes of today's media usually win, not because of the power of good over evil, but because of their greater ability to be violent. Thus James Bond, Indiana Jones and even Batman all win through by the strength of the gun, the horsewhip, and the fist – 'POW!!'

3.22   A further component in many films and videos is the portrayal of evil and the occult. A film like *Ghostbusters* may handle this in a light-hearted and humorous manner but many films portray horror and evil as an attraction with the risk of either causing trauma or, alternatively, desensitising a child's resistance to the violent and the frightening. Already school teachers are commenting on an increasing incidence of violence in the playground.

In May 1987 the National Association of Head Teachers discussed how to cope with mounting violence in the classroom. A newspaper report in *The Observer* contained these words: 'Mr Martin Saunders, head of St Thomas' Primary School, Stoke, said last week he was receiving complaints from other heads that five- and six-year-olds were involved in karate chopping, head butting and kneeing other children in the groin. Some were even kicking teachers. He added: "A large number of children are now coming from broken homes. They are being subject to violence and they are seeing violence in their families. They are watching more unsupervised television."'[5]

Violence also extends to language. Four-letter words are now part of the stock-in-trade of most film heroes, including the teenage central figure of the brilliant *Back to the Future* series.

3.23   Another disturbing component of much of what enters children's experience from television is a disdain for authority. In this area we have to exercise some care, for every generation has tended to bemoan a growing lack of respect with regard to young people:

The world is passing through troublous times. The young people of today think of nothing but themselves. They have no reverence for parents or old age. They are impatient of all restraint. They talk as if they knew everything, and what passes for wisdom with us is foolishness to them. As for girls, they are immodest and unwomanly in speech, behaviour and dress. *(Peter the Hermit, c.* AD 1050-1115.)

3.24   Pop groups often depict in their style and music a defiance towards existing norms. Many child-centred programmes take for granted a certain conspiracy against older generations, and loyalty to parents is not always very obvious. In *The Assault on Childhood,* Ron Goulart writes:

> In our present situation, adulthood has lost much of its authority and aura, and the idea of deference to one who is older has become ridiculous. [6]

There can be a certain healthiness in all this. Children are entitled to know the reasons behind rules and regulations and some such rules in schools and homes can exist merely for the convenience of adults. However, any healthy society needs people who can understand the reason for law, order and the place of authority.

OUTSIDE INFLUENCES – COMMERCIAL TARGETING

3.25   The report *Children in the Way* identified a second major area of pressure and influence:

> The commercial world bombards quite small children with television advertisements for toys, for example; the promotion of children's fashions in clothes encourages the child to choose what he or she wants and to make those decisions clear. [7]

3.26   In the mid-eighties unemployment among school-leavers rose sharply after a long period when this age group had been targeted as a buying elite. Consequently the emphasis of commercial interest has shifted towards the younger child (relying on the more certain income of his or her parents). Whole new industries have developed entirely because of this shift of emphasis and old established ones traditionally selling into the younger children's market have flourished.

3.27   David Porter[8] points out that 24 per cent of all sales in the multi-million pound toy market are Teddy Bears. However, the new phenomenon of the past three decades is the 'collectable' character doll or toy – 'Barbie', 'Sindy', 'My Little Pony', 'Robocop', 'Manta Force', 'Thundercats' and many others. These dolls are each the focus of an ever growing range of accessories with the accompanying pressure on parents to buy and help the child collect the full set. Some of these 'collectables' are linked into their own comics and even videos drawn from their US television shows.

3.28 Writing about the 1989/1990 promotion of 'Teenage Mutant Hero Turtles' (who are supposed to live in sewers) Maggie Brown, Media correspondent of *The Independent,* identified the commercialism that cloaked itself in children's entertainment:

> My objections to the Turtles are not based on their impact on children's behaviour. It is something quite different. The Turtles are an example of how, on the back of TV programmes, a world-wide media marketing machine is able to flood homes with Turtle mugs, bubble-bath, books, comic strips, duvet covers and T-shirts. Sensible children build pretend sewers in their bedrooms. They don't go down the real ones. But it takes a very tough parent and a very unworldly child to hold out against the Turtle sell.[9]

3.29 Barbie and Sindy dolls are not the dolls of 30 years ago. They have contemporary hair styles, wasp-like waists and long, shapely legs. They are every little girl's fantasy of what she would like to be. They have glamorous clothes and sensational hairstyles – *they are about life style.* With the life style comes a set of values, a statement by implication about what things are to be sought after in life: fine clothes, good hair, a slim figure, a horse of one's own, holidays in Spain, exotic night clubs and rock venues. Even for young children it is vital to know the latest trends in clothes and hairstyles – a seven-year-old boy can be humiliated if he has to wear an unfashionable garment in front of his peers.

3.30 Very many of today's children have their own computer or have access to one in the home. It is used mainly as a games machine. Most of the video games available in pubs and arcades are available in versions for home micros. As in pop music, there are peer pressures to be playing the latest games. The benefit of computer literacy is a great gain as against saturation television watching. The other side of the coin is that computer activity is hardly a social event. As in so many activities such as watching TV and using a Walkman, relating to other people is not necessary. The message and the morality of the games are not discussed or evaluated. They are simply taken on board.

3.31 Many computer games have a war and destruction theme, as do many boys' collectables. This ties in with other components of the huge menu of toys on offer each Christmas time. *Guardian* columnist Jill Tweedie has written:

Christmas should be about loved ones and families, glad tidings and goodwill to all mankind and, above all, peace on earth... And, still nodding agreement, you know what most of us do then? To honour the Prince of Peace, the man who said suffer the little children to come unto Me, we rush out and buy our little children the instruments of war and sudden death. Rubber swords, plastic daggers, throwing knives, rifles, hand grenades, helmets, games to do with skilful killing and, above all, tons and tons of guns.[10]

3.32 It must be acknowledged immediately that there is more than one school of thought on the harmfulness or otherwise of toy guns and swords. What must be recognised, however, *is the high-powered commercialism in the toy industry*. It is backed by skilful television advertising. It is often tied in to movies, TV series and comics. Children can become totally caught up in the pursuit of more and more expensive components to make up the full set of this or that highly promoted range. The child is the victim of and could be the convert to – *materialism*. It is hardly an object lesson in learning that 'man does not live by bread alone'.

3.33 There are two by-products of the commercial assault upon today's children. The first is the mobilisation of peer group pressure and the second is the promotion of role models. There is often a necessary connection between the two.

3.34 In terms of clothing and footwear, sports heroes are identified with 'designer' clothes and feature in advertising for those garments. At this point peer pressure comes into play to increase the incentive to be seen wearing the 'right gear'.

3.35 Children need heroes and they find them projected into their lives through the alliance between showbusiness, sport and commerce. The problem is that heroes have changed over the years. Today's hero is light years away from the world of *The Boys Own Paper* or even Walt Disney. It can be a soccer player who commits the professional foul when required, Indiana Jones who bullwhips his enemies, or the latest rock star whose lyrics may be full of aggression, whose life style may hint at drugs and who makes no secret of life with his latest live-in girl friend.

3.36 One of the more disturbing developments during the 1980s has been the boom in fantasy games, books and computer programmes for children. The Fantasy Role Play (FRP) encouraged in this material has a well-defined structure of good versus evil. The message it carries can be summarised as follows:

1. The human race needs someone or something bigger and stronger than itself to deal with its problems.
2. If you summon supernatural help your problem will always be solved.
3. The force of 'Good' is a mysterious, impersonal power.

If a child is receiving the impression on a daily basis (these games are compulsive) that evil is defeated through strength, what will be the long-term effects of such indoctrination?

3.37 FRP magazines have circulations of 50,000 upwards and the hobby clearly appeals to those of 10 years upwards. 'Dungeons and Dragons' can have an addictive effect and educates children into the workings of the occult and the supernaturally evil. David Porter in *Children at Risk* [11] argues that there is a real danger that the children playing such games will want to explore occult practices as a result. For those who would ask if there was much difference between FRP material and some of the more gruesome fairy tales of old, the answer is that we are dealing with something of a totally different order. The books are full of illustrations of human sacrifices, vampires and ghouls, agonised figures chained to dungeon walls, semi-human creatures with long talons for fingers and so on. It is difficult to know what is more disturbing, the thought of children being deeply frightened by this material or the thought of them finding it entertaining! What needs to be remembered at all times is that this is *role-play* material, involving the reader's imagination and asking them to make decisions about action which is often violent.

HOW SHOULD THE CHURCHES RESPOND?

3.38 It is extremely difficult to prove that particular influences in a culture will lead to consequences in terms of people's conduct. (This has been recognised in the long-running debate as to whether pornography affects behaviour.) It is also very easy to write up the world of today's child in alarmist terms. Fortunately very many children belong to stable families with clear sets of values. The influence of Christianity still affects the way many seek to bring up their children. Further, the child can be remarkably resilient and – as many teachers and parents are apt to lament – astonishingly impervious to the suggestions of others. Nevertheless elements in our society are combining to create for today's children a prematurely adult and somewhat lonely world that accustoms them to materialism, hedonism, selfishness, sexual amorality, the unseriousness and even normality of violence, the possibility of spiritual power through an openness to the occult – and all this against an ever-weakening acknowledgement of the truth and relevance of Christianity.

3.39 To have qualms about evangelising children because of a worthy fear of pressurising the immature means that they are left to wallow in a world of false values and gospels – others have few such qualms!

3.40 To concentrate evangelism upon adults or even those in adolescence, is to ignore the possibility that existing social pressures and assumptions might have already shaped and hardened an alternative belief system in young people which will be harder to counter.

3.41 Above all, to do nothing for those children whose parents don't come to church is to acquiesce to their setting out on life with no memories or openness to the story of Jesus who is the way, the truth and the life. For the established Church of the realm to organise itself in such a way that it shows no concern for the spiritual welfare of the nation's children is to betray its historic vocation. To bond together with other Christians and call ourselves the 'Churches Together in England' and yet to practise disinterest in the children of England is surely unthinkable.

3.42 The Working Party is convinced that the Churches must – as a matter of urgency – invest new energies and resources into the evangelism of those millions of children at present beyond the reach of any congregation. We need to attempt to be a major contributor in the market place of experiences within which today's children live. This is not something that the Churches can take in their stride – it calls for a fundamental change. It also calls for the facing of a number of difficult social, pastoral and theological questions and to these we shall now turn.

4 Facing the Issues

... in biblical societies (especially Israel) the family was a self-supporting economic, social and spiritual unit in itself. Those who call for a return to biblical patterns of family must recognise the very different world in which we live. (Francis Bridger, *Children Finding Faith* (Scripture Union, 1988), p. 140.)

Let the little children come to me, and do not hinder them, for the Kingdom of God belongs to such as these. (Mark 10.14.)

4.1   Any discussion of evangelising the children of people who do not themselves attend church raises a number of theological and pastoral questions. In this chapter we shall discuss:

1.   Does God have a focused concern for children in themselves outside of the family? There are many who would hold that it is, somehow, 'unbiblical' to attempt to minister to children outside of the family unit.
2.   Is 'evangelism' an appropriate thing to do with children? Are we not in danger of putting unfair pressure upon a vulnerable group?
3.   How should the churches relate to the parents of those children who take part in their activities? Is there not a danger of conspiring with the children against their parents?
4.   How do churches handle a situation where children from other faith communities attend their gospel-sharing activities?
5.   How do we relate children's evangelism to baptism and confirmation?

CHILDREN AND GOD

4.2   There is no record of children being converted in the Acts of the Apostles. There are, however, several references to the conversion of entire 'households' based on the personal attitude of the family head (e.g. Acts 16.15; 16.34; 18.8). The impression given is that the child's stand-

34

ing before God is locked into the attitude of the parents. This would appear to square with the picture of family spirituality in the Old Testament also.

4.3   In the Old Testament the birth of children is a matter of great rejoicing, and barrenness a matter of despair or even reproach:

> Sons are a heritage from the Lord,
> children a reward from him.
> Like arrows in the hands of a warrior
> are the sons born in one's youth.
> Blessed is the man
> whose quiver is full of them.
> They will not be put to shame
> when they contend with their enemies in the gate.
>
> (Psalm 127.3ff.)

In these words one quickly notes a certain lack of romanticism. There is no sense of drooling over babies. Offspring are about safety and security for the family and the tribe. They are also about the continuing of the line.

4.4   Hans-Reudi Weber in his book *Jesus and the Children* states: '... the Israelites did not idealise children, nor did they pay any special attention to the children's individuality'.[1] Much of this can be explained in the light of the social context of Old Testament times. There was no such thing as the modern state or the local authority providing education, health care or policing. People banded together in their 'extended families' (which included household servants) for physical and economic survival.

4.5   In this setting obedience to parents was seen as an extremely serious matter. The welfare of large numbers of people depended on strong family loyalty. The fifth commandment bears witness to this. Parental discipline could be strict ('He who spares the rod hates his son') and in the case of a totally rebellious son there was even a provision for the men of the town to stone him to death (Deut. 21.18ff).

4.6   Before the Exile there were no schools or any sort of religious education for children. They learnt respect for God and his law and saw their place in the story of the nation that had been led out of Egypt – all from their parents. This being the case, the parents were held responsible for the proper discharge of these religious responsibilities, as the sad story of Eli and his sons bears witness (1 Sam. 3 and 4).

4.7   In the late twentieth century families are usually 'nuclear' and independent. The differing generations team up with their peers and, at times, have an existence that is independent of others in the family. Only in remote farming areas are there any examples of the differing generations of families needing each other economically and physically. Schooling of children is done in peer groups and practically nobody would want things any other way. To point to the Bible and claim that the only correct way to minister to children is in the context of the family is to confuse divine command with the particular culture of biblical times.

4.8   Nor must it be forgotten that in the Old Testament children did have religious significance. The rite of entry into the Covenant relationship, circumcision, took place on the eighth day of a boy's life. Children were brought up as insiders and included in worship at home and in the great celebrations of the Covenant. Again the Old Testament records instances of children who exercised genuine ministry to the whole community. Samuel is a classic case as is Joash (2 Kings 12) who began his honourable reign at the age of seven. The servant girl of Naaman (2 Kings 5) is also singled out as someone used by God in an adult world.

4.9   The Gospels show Jesus growing up in a society little different from that pictured in the Old Testament. The incident described in Luke 2.41-52 reveals the breadth of the extended family. Mary and Joseph assume that the boy Jesus must be with other relatives or friends on their return from Jerusalem, before discovering otherwise. He is rebuked for not regarding his father's wishes (v.48) only to hint at a more profound relationship with another father.

Indeed the closeness of the family unit is later shown by Christ to be of secondary importance to the new family created around 'whoever does God's will...' (Mark 3.31-35). While the Lord's loyalty and concern for his mother should not be questioned – he was anxious for her welfare even when dying (John 19.25-27) – he always held that the claims of the gospel were bigger than family ties. 'Anyone who loves his father or his mother more than me is not worthy of me ...' (Matt. 10.37). To have a desire to reach whole families for Christ must surely be good. To limit one's outreach to such a vision, however, is to ignore an aspect of Christ's own teaching.

4.10   The Jesus described in the Gospels was obviously liked by children and clearly showed an affection for them. 'George Macdonald used to say that no man could be a follower of Jesus if the children were afraid to play at his door. Jesus was certainly no grim ascetic if the children loved him.'[2] This is all the more remarkable because of the common attitude of Rabbis towards children.

Weber states: 'For a scholar to play with children and spend time with them outside his teaching period was regarded as a waste of time.' This, anyhow, was the opinion of Rabbi Dosa ben Harkinas (*c.* AD 90) which is reported in the *Mishna*: 'Morning sleep and mid-day wine and children's talk and sitting in the meeting houses of ignorant people put a man out of the world.'[3]

4.11 Children are recorded, on several occasions, as being near Jesus in the crowds. The boy with the loaves and fishes was obviously close at hand (John 6.9). When Jesus (Matt. 18.2) called a little child to come to him, and used that child as a model of humility and trustfulness, the child was obviously within range. As George Macdonald would have put it, children were not 'afraid to play at his door'. In Matthew 21.15,16 we read of children in the Temple chanting the Lord's praise. Clearly he made an impact on them which would not have happened if he had not taken them seriously.

4.12 Probably the key passage in the Gospels is that recorded in Mark 10.13-16 (paralleled in Matt. 19 and Luke 18):

> People were bringing little children to Jesus to have him touch them, but the disciples rebuked them. When Jesus saw this, he was indignant. He said to them, 'Let the little children come to me, and do not hinder them, for the kingdom of God belongs to such as these. I tell you the truth, anyone who will not receive the kingdom of God like a little child will never enter it.' And he took the children in his arms, put his hands on them and blessed them.

Apart from the fact that Jesus obviously showed affection towards the children, how are we to understand the phrase: 'the kingdom of heaven belongs to such as these'? Some have tried to argue from these words that children have a special standing with God and that they are therefore automatically 'insiders' until they opt out. This, however, is to read too much into the words and to ignore the context.

Others would argue that Jesus (as in Matt. 18.1-4) is using the children as an object lesson to teach his followers about the need for humility. This view is given some support in Mark's and Luke's account where, unlike the parallel in Matthew, they include the words about the need to receive the kingdom of God like a little child.

A key word in the passage is: 'such'. Jesus is making an important point to his followers who thought he was too busy and too important to have time for toddlers. The Lord's rejoinder is that the kingdom (which was at the heart of all his teaching) actually *belonged* to such insignificant persons as toddlers. The Lord's words are spoken with feeling. He was indignant at the attitude of his followers.

The distinguished German theologian Jürgen Moltmann sees the children not only as examples of humility but as examples of the 'poor' and powerless in society for whom Christ particularly came and who had an instinctive recognition of his kingdom values:

> The gospel does not merely bring the kingdom of God to the poor: it also discovers the kingdom of the poor which is God's kingdom.... It also shows that the poor are God's fellow citizens, like the children to whom the kingdom of God already belongs.... According to Jesus' gospel, the kingdom of God is already present among the poor and the sick and among the children and slaves of the people.[4]

It is probable that – as with the parables – Jesus did not intend his words to have a precise meaning. Rather they were intended to trigger a number of insights in his hearers to the new values and perspectives that follow from accepting his reign over our affairs. What is clear is that not only did Jesus personally enjoy the company of children, he believed that they mattered to God and that it was appropriate for them to enjoy his presence and blessing.

4.13 No discussion of the teaching and action of Jesus regarding children should be separated from the fact that he was, himself, for many years, a child. The Incarnation is a statement about God's identification with and hallowing of humanity. But to say that 'the Word became flesh' can cover up the implication that the Word, for some time, became a child. The second century Bishop of Lyons, Irenaeus, saw this more clearly than most:

> ... he came to save all through himself; all, that is, who through him are born into God, infants, children, boys, young men and old. Therefore he passed through every stage of life: he was made an infant for infants, sanctifying infancy; a child among children, sanctifying those of this age; an example also to them of filial affection, righteousness and obedience....[5]

4.14 The Working Party concluded from its reflection upon Scripture that a specific ministry towards children – conducted with due respect

for their family ties and with a sensitive realism as to their vulnerability – is entirely appropriate. Further, they concluded that such a
ministry was necessary in a society where the differing generations, even
in united families, spend a great deal of time in the company of their
peers. They also felt that concern for the well-being of children, physical
and spiritual, was a mark of the very kingdom that Christ announced. By
his person and by his personality Jesus revealed that God is *for* children.

SHOULD WE EVANGELISE?

4.15 'There was a part of me', writes Rebecca Manley Pippert in her
book *Out of the Saltshaker,* 'that secretly felt evangelism was something
you shouldn't do to your dog, let alone a friend'.[6] In spite of the fact that
Church leaders have endorsed the Decade of Evangelism, there remain
many reservations in the pews. For some 'evangelism' means forcing
one's views on others. For some it is associated with sloganising about
God to people who may, or may not, be interested. Even serious newspapers confuse 'Evangelical' (a theological tradition) with 'Evangelist'
(someone whose ministry is to explain and commend the gospel). In recent years the term 'televangelist' has been coined to describe flamboyant
American television preachers, some of whom became caught up in much
publicised scandals. (The Working Party set up to report on children's
evangelism was even urged by some to drop the word.)

4.16 Even those who believe in the importance of evangelism are apt to
describe it as 'preaching the gospel in such a way that people are brought
to belief'. This on the one hand encourages pictures of standing on soap
boxes preaching in stylised ways with little place for listening; and on the
other hand hints at putting emotional pressure on people to make them
change their beliefs.

4.17 The word 'evangelism' does not, of necessity, imply any of these
things. It is made up of two parts, the main part is 'evangel' (meaning
good news); while the suffix 'ism' refers to procedures, actions and
systems that are appropriate to the main part of the word. So evangelism
means *activities designed to help people discover the good news.*

4.18 The Working Party found two current definitions of evangelism
helpful, the first from the 1987 BMU/PWM report *The Measure of Mission,*[7] and the second coming from William Abraham's timely book *The
Logic of Evangelism.*[8] (The Working Party could not help noticing that

39

The Measure of Mission begins with a case study of ten instances of mission and that not one of the ten was centred upon children's ministry.)

4.19 In *The Measure of Mission* there is an extended description of how the word 'evangelism' should be understood. The heart of the section is contained in the following sentences:

> Evangelism is the making known of the gospel of the Lord Jesus Christ, especially to those who do not know it.... We are charged to communicate that the life, death and resurrection of Jesus Christ is good news from God. Evangelism usually involves the use of words, but not inevitably so. Identification and solidarity with people are indispensable and may themselves be forms of evangelism if they evoke a response which enables Jesus Christ to be named. Much communication takes place at a non-verbal level and even the verbal has a visual aspect and can have other forms of expression added to it: drama, music, dance, mime or symbolic action. It is essential in evangelism that the dignity of human beings is affirmed by giving them freedom to choose, without pressure.... Certainly it is the hope of evangelists that their hearers will be persuaded and come to faith....[9]

The first strength of this definition is that it focuses upon the story to be told and the telling of it. Some definitions speak too much of what is held to be the object of the exercise (such as conversion and incorporation into the Church). Here the stress is truly upon the *evangel* – the life, death and resurrection of Jesus Christ (cf. 1 Cor. 15.1-8). This is what, in this report and especially in the next chapter, is called 'the story'. In children's evangelism the concept of evangelism that is most satisfactory is 'story-orientated' rather than 'response-orientated'. So much of what we may be doing is investing in the future – building in lasting memories of the story and the people who told it.

The second strength of this definition is that it avoids a commitment to any particular means of communication. Rather than talk of 'proclaiming the gospel' – with all the associations of preaching *at* people – it settles for 'making known ... the gospel'. The Lambeth Conference Resolution 43 concerning the Decade of Evangelism also uses this helpful form of words. The value of this terminology is that one can focus at least as much on how people *receive* the information as on how others may *impart* it. Too much discussion of evangelism is weighted on the 'retailer' end of the equation rather than the 'consumer' end. In children's evangelism (and surely this ought to apply to any type of evangelism) it is important to reflect upon *how people discover the gospel for themselves*. In the majority of cases the discovery is made as a result of a process of experiences and encounters – of which direct story telling is usually but not always one component.

The third strength of this definition lies in its emphasis upon 'identification and solidarity' as indispensable and as having an evangelistic effect in themselves. We are talking here about the incarnational aspect of evangelism. Disembodied messages can never replace the presence of message bearers. In children's work this is especially important. It is often Christ seen in the person of a leader that communicates and remains in the memory. Again 'solidarity' matters. An ill-resourced club or Sunday gathering staffed by a lone enthusiast or two, is no evidence of the congregation's solidarity with children. The plea of the Working Party is that the body language of the congregation should speak of the welcome and the importance given to the children of the neighbourhood.

The fourth strength of this definition lies in its respect for the dignity and vulnerability of those being evangelised. This should always be the case but it is a particularly crucial matter when we contemplate evangelising children and especially the children of those who do not attend church. It is very easy to sway children – particularly when they are members of a crowd. Manipulation is all too easy and very often it is completely unintentional. An enthusiastic young adult talking attractively to a group of children who have just laughed and sung heartily can evoke a response to whatever he or she is angling for, that may seem genuine at the time, but soon afterwards will be seen to be spurious. More seriously, some ways of handling themes like judgement can disturb sensitive children for prolonged periods of time.

The fifth strength of this definition is that, in spite of fully recognising the danger of exerting false pressures, it acknowledges the great hope that lies behind all evangelism. The 'hope of evangelists' is that 'their hearers will be persuaded and come to faith'. That hope should be the foundation of their prayers but it needs to be informed by a realism. The reality is that while children can easily 'make decisions', these, while sincere, are often fleeting. What children's evangelisers need to keep in mind is a longer term scenario. Rather than seeking to achieve an adult type response now, what we long for is *an adult type of response to Christ when the children are adults.* There are appropriate responses for children to make and these will be discussed in the next chapter, but many of these relate to identification with the group or community in what it is saying or doing.

41

4.20   The definition of evangelism reached by Dr William Abraham in *The Logic of Evangelism* opens up a further important concern:

> We can best improve our thinking on evangelism by conceiving it as that set of intentional activities which is governed by the goal of initiating people into the kingdom of God for the first time. [10]

The first strength in this way of defining evangelism lies in the recognition of a 'set of intentional activities'. Once again we are moved away from focusing narrowly on preaching or even the use of words at all. Very often in children's or youth evangelism youngsters come alive to the faith of the group as they become involved in a series of activities, many of them recreational. The intention behind such activities, however, is that through enjoying the company of Christians and through occasional informal discussions, the child or young person discerns the 'Christian difference' that characterises the group. The creation of such a context for inter-relationships can be properly described as 'evangelistic' because it is 'governed by the goal of initiating people into the kingdom for the first time'.

The second great strength of this definition – and it is more fully developed in his book – is that Abraham recognises that what is often described as 'nurture' is, in practice, inseparable from evangelism. It is the view of the Working Party that children's evangelism is largely a nurturing activity. One of the most significant developments in recent evangelistic practice, affecting churches of differing traditions, is the recognition that nurture and 'discovery group' models seem to be the most effective ways of helping people to discover the gospel and respond to it. Children are no exception.

4.21   The Working Party recognised from its discussions that the 'doing' of evangelism was about the creation of formats and contexts within which people can discover the gospel for themselves. This understanding has much in common with some descriptions of the educational process and in particular the evangelism of children needs to be seen in terms of education rather than persuasion.

KEEPING FAITH WITH THE PARENTS

4.22   Christians place great emphasis on the value of family life. How can they be true to this emphasis in situations where they have access to children whose parents give no indication of sympathy towards

Christianity and may even be hostile? There is a moral question here. Is it right to set up a rival for the affections and loyalty of the child towards his or her parents? Is there a danger of creating division in other people's homes?

4.23   In addition to the moral question there is a practical and strategic issue. We have seen from the first chapter that in the heyday of the Sunday school the retention of children who came without parents into adult church membership was abysmal, at best about one in twenty. There are strong voices who would urge us to concentrate on reaching whole families and to doubt the wisdom of investing resources into the 'failed strategy' of trying to reach children apart from their parents.

4.24   The response to this criticism must be to challenge the assumption that low levels of subsequent adult church attendance are evidence of a failed strategy. In some sections of English society there have been strong social customs that virtually ruled out adult church attendance. Nevertheless such communities often displayed belief in God, a readiness to turn to the Churches in times of need and a moral outlook clearly influenced by Christian values. All those spiritual and moral traits must have been developed through childhood association with Sunday schools.

4.25   There is no way of measuring the real and residual faith that the old Sunday schools implanted in their pupils in the earlier decades of this century. Many a priest and pastor will testify to the influence that memories of childhood faith have upon people in later life. In reaching out to children we are 'casting bread upon the waters' and we must believe that there will be a return of some good sort in later days both within the later experiences of the children reached, and within the congregations of the future. As we have seen in Chapter 1, there are good grounds for believing that children's ministry in past years has, to a significant degree, filtered through to church membership in later years.

4.26   School teachers know, however, that the children who learn and grow to their full potential at any stage are usually those with a stable and supportive home environment. The good school will seek the maximum acceptance and, if possible, active support of the home.

4.27   It is possible to overstate the matter of parental antipathy or indifference towards belief in God. Polls regularly reveal that over 70 per cent of the population claim to believe in God. Only some 15 per cent are prepared to call themselves atheists. A common answer to the question

'Would you encourage your children to go to church activities' is: *'If they want to go, I wouldn't stop them.'* That answer may reveal less conviction than the answers given 35 years ago to such researchers as Gorer but it hardly constitutes a veto against the sort of evangelism we have been describing in this chapter.

4.28 Churches attempting to evangelise the children of non-attending parents need to regard those parents as allies until the evidence suggests otherwise. They should seek to conspire *with* them about the spiritual development of their children rather than to conspire *against* them. There are many indicators to suggest that large numbers of parents are concerned that their children should have a Christian, or at least religious, experience as part of their overall education about life. Many non-practising adults would use the word 'Christian' to describe themselves and are perfectly happy for local churches to provide activities for their children where they can learn about the Christian faith.

4.29 We should seek to evangelise children in a spirit of coming alongside their parents rather than that of coming against them. Several guidelines should help this to happen.

1. Only share with children what you can share with their parents.
2. Encourage children to tell their parents what they have done or learned or care about.
3. Do not encourage a 'defiant spirit' – a feeling of superiority in the child over his parents because he is, or is becoming, a Christian.
4. Keep a steady flow of information to the parents.
5. Set up family opportunities – outings, parents' evenings, etc.
6. Always seek parental support and approval.

To seek specific permissions is unrealistic but a golden rule of any evangelistic exercise, be it Sunday school, a holiday club, beach mission or club night, is that parents must be informed so that at least their agreement can be presumed.

CHILDREN IN MULTI-FAITH CONTEXTS

4.30 So far we have considered only those children whose families have some kind of background, however vestigial, of Christian faith. It is the church that they stay away from, not the mosque or temple or the synagogue. But what of the children whose family traditions, whether closely or loosely observed, link them with one of the other world faiths?

4.31   There are many issues here, sociological and theological. First, it needs to be said that such children are likely to be much more members of communities than their (mostly white) counterparts. In this document we have so far mainly referred to the family unit as comprising simply parents and children. With the Muslim, Hindu and Sikh communities in particular we have to think in terms of much larger family and community units. It is uncles and aunts and grandparents who will have an effective say in the nurture of children as well as parents. Where religious affiliation is concerned, whole communities may feel threatened if vulnerable members, like children, are 'enticed' away from them. Adult or adolescent members of such communities who show an active interest in Christian faith have often experienced hostility amounting to real persecution from their families. Those who accept baptism have sometimes been totally excluded from the family circle and even regarded as dead. It is easy therefore to imagine the resentment which may be felt at attempts to 'corrupt' children of such families.

4.32   At the same time the situation in Britain is far from uniform. The extended family system has proved much more difficult to sustain in this country than in the countries of origin, and many Asian parents fear that their children will lose their inherited culture altogether. Some parents may prefer a definite Christian influence on their children than no religious influence at all. This is the reason for many Asian parents choosing to send their children to a Church school. However, they do not usually anticipate or welcome the prospect of their children actually becoming Christians as a result.

4.33   All this should give pause for thought to those who would see all children, of whatever background, as equally appropriate recipients of evangelism. If the Church has a mission to the Hindu, Jewish, Muslim and Sikh communities, as surely it has, it does not want to threaten those communities by appearing to attack them, targeting their weakest and most cherished members.

4.34   Theologically there is currently great debate on the theological status in Christian eyes of other world faiths. This is unlikely to be resolved in the near future. Perhaps it can be said that neither of the extreme views – that other faiths are the products of Satanic influence, and that they are simply alternative roads to the same goal – have found much favour in official Church documents. The 1984 document *Towards a Theology for Inter-Faith Dialogue,* which became one of the preparatory papers for the 1988 Lambeth Conference, states that the authors:

> ... expect that God will speak to us through the sensitivities and experiences of devout men and women of other faiths. We expect our own faith to be challenged, refined and at times judged, but we are firm in our loyalty to the revelation of God in and through the life, death and resurrection of Jesus of Nazareth... We discover that it is out of weakness and not strength that we make our witness and our appeal. [11]

4.35   If it is out of such weakness and not out of strength that we make our witness, then God will surely honour our faithfulness in speaking to children, as to others, of what we know and believe about him. We should not attempt to control or shape their response. This may well be the right way in which to approach all children; it certainly seems right for children of other faiths.

A PLACE FOR BAPTISM?

4.36   If we are to understand evangelism amongst children as something that is mainly to do with education and nurture, what place should we have for baptism? For several years the number of children being baptised has been dropping. In 1950, 67 per cent of all live births were followed by baptism. In ten years the numbers had dropped to 55 per cent. By 1980 the figure stood at 38 per cent and by 1987 this number had dropped further to 29 per cent. (Similarly confirmation figures have declined from 191,000 in 1960 – in the era of the 'baby boom' – to 98,000 in 1980 and 64,000 in 1988.) If the churches are to increase significantly their outreach to the children of non-attenders they will find themselves dealing with large numbers of unbaptised children.

4.37   What then should our attitude be to an unbaptised child who gives every sign of believing the story of Christ and enjoying being part of the Christian community? If Jesus claimed that the kingdom of God belonged to such as these, should we not be offering the sacrament of baptism? (Obviously this is a particular dilemma for churches that practise infant baptism, but those who practise 'believer's baptism' might also find this a testing question in the case of a mature 13-year-old girl who appears to have found a strong faith in spite of the absence of parental support.)

4.38   The Working Party believed that this was a matter for very great caution. The baptism of children without full parental encouragement would surely be ill advised. However, if good links had been formed with the families and such cases of apparently strong belief occurred, there might well be grounds for suggesting to the parents that they consider requesting baptism for their child. Should this be taken up, such children ought to be given particular support from the children's activity leaders – not least at the Baptism Service.

4.39   While it is probably right to make provision for baptism in particular instances following the request of parents, the Working Party did not believe that seeking the baptism of the unbaptised should be a major objective of the sort of children's evangelism which they envisaged.

SUMMARY

4.40   So, to summarise, the Working Party's study of scripture underlined the appropriateness of a ministry aimed specifically at children. Such a concern reflected their view of the kingdom that Christ announced, of which efforts to enable children to grow spiritually as well as physically are a particular mark.

4.41   This ministry to children can be called 'doing evangelism', and is about creating contexts within which people can discover the gospel. This approach fits well with current educational methods, as does the need to work alongside the children's parents as partners in the process of nurture.

4.42   Finally, in this chapter we have considered the problems and opportunities facing us when working with children from homes and backgrounds of other faiths or of no faith. Here, as indeed with all our work of evangelism, we believe that God will recognise our faithfulness in speaking of what we know and believe about him, and will honour our desire to do so without attempting to control or shape people's response. In the end we must leave God the Holy Spirit to work in and through all our work of evangelism, and we must leave him free to work as he wills.

5 What Sort of Evangelism?

In a children's mission, where it is possible to have a good number of unchurched children, it is soon obvious that the ones who are easiest and
soonest bored are the church children, while outsiders are excited by, and en-
thralled with, the stories of Jesus. (Comment from a full-time children's
worker.)

5.1 Evangelism never takes place in a vacuum. There is always
something 'there' before it occurs. In the case of the parish church in
England there is a great deal that is already 'there'. Again evangelism is
best seen – in the local church context – not so much as a special activity but rather as a vision and dimension that pervades all congregational
activities as well as the life style of the members.

EVANGELISM WITHIN MISSION

5.2 Evangelism is 'a particular responsibility in the Church's mission'.[1]
As such it benefits from being 'of a piece' with all other outgoing expres-
sions to the community of the love of God.

Children's evangelism is likely to benefit from being 'of a piece' with a
welcoming, sensitive baptismal policy which has faithful after-care. It
will likewise be enhanced if it is part of a church's outreach that shows
concern for parents with young children, especially with the growing
need to help mothers who must return to work as soon as possible after
childbirth. (There is a great danger that churches could stand back
critically at such a development rather than recognise that here is a need
to be met.)

Again, the evangelism of children is likely to be enhanced in a church
which seeks to forge creative links with local schools.

5.3 Evangelism does not have to wait upon central policy decisions. If
every churchgoing family developed the habit of inviting friends of their
children to join them at the appropriate church services, the overall
evangelistic impact might be considerable.

5.4   Evangelism is not a one-way, patronising activity. Consideration of the gospel evangelises both the sharer and the receiver. Again, when it comes to the evangelism of children of non-attending parents (as we have seen in Chapter 4) we should not assume hostility or even disinterest on the part of the parents. Many such parents believe that an awareness of Christian teaching is good for their children. Some are themselves lapsed, and seeing their children getting involved in the church makes them feel less 'guilty'.

BASIC ASSUMPTIONS

5.5   Having said this, there are a number of assumptions that we cannot make in this sort of children's evangelism.

1. We cannot assume parental support or encouragement.
2. We cannot assume our activities will lead to eventual church affiliation.
3. We cannot assume any previous knowledge of the Bible.
4. We cannot assume that we will have contexts and opportunities for the orderly presentation of the gospel.
5. We cannot assume emotional maturity in the children or that all children will receive with the same openness or level of understanding.

5.6.   There are, however, a number of assumptions that it is possible to make.

1. We can assume that most children will respond to genuine *love.*
2. We can assume that children are likely to show an openness to God.
3. We can assume that our Lord is deeply concerned for children and that his Spirit is with us.
4. We can assume that there is some profound meaning to the Lord's words that the kingdom belongs to children.
5. We can assume that children can grasp the concept of Jesus as a 'special friend'.

FAITH DEVELOPMENT AND EVANGELISM

5.7   The report, *Children in the Way,* made reference to the Faith Development school of thought with which scholars such as John Westerhoff and James Fowler are associated. While not accepting their thinking uncritically, it acknowledged the value of Faith Development insights.[2] These recognise that, as with physical development, so faith shows a process of growth and that this is something different from purely intellectual development. If evangelism is about awakening faith in the living story of Jesus, then any insights into the ways that faith develops are likely to prove helpful.

5.8 Westerhoff describes a development process through four 'styles of faith'. He draws an analogy with tree rings. As the tree grows, new rings are added but none are eliminated. People develop from one style of faith to another as a result of their experience and encounters. The four styles which Westerhoff identifies are as follows:

1. *Experienced Faith.* This is little more than an acceptance of and readiness to trust all that surrounds the young child. If the family life style is focused upon faith in Christ, then the manifestations of that – such as bedtime prayer – are simply taken on board uncritically as the norm. If there is no such religious faith, then the child's trust system will have no such focus.

2. *Affiliative Faith.* As the child becomes aware of the community to which he or she belongs, there is a natural tendency to accept the beliefs and value systems of that community. If it is a Christian fellowship then it is what Westerhoff calls 'an identity-conscious community of faith'. Religious feelings in the child are nurtured through sharing in the community's activities of worship and story-telling. The child (or adult, as this stage can last for years) takes up the beliefs and attitudes of the group and greatly values the sense of belonging to it.

3. *Searching Faith.* This third style describes the person who is moving on from uncritical acceptance of the faith of the affiliation. There is a desire to be rid of outside authority and a feeling that any faith worth having must be personal. There will be times of doubt, criticism, even rebellion against the affiliation. There will be the need to experiment and the inevitability of what will later be seen as mistakes. What needs to be remembered is that this jumble of intellectual, experimental and even moral responses is still a *style of faith.*

4. *Owned Faith.* This describes the point that people can reach when they know for themselves why and what they believe. It is the end of a conversion experience which is, usually, 'a long pilgrimage', although there can be times of sudden discovery within the process.

5.9   Taking Westerhoff's analysis we must ask *what is the style of faith appropriate to focus upon in the evangelism of children who have no apparent parental support?* The answer must surely seem to be: *that of affiliative faith.* We should want every child possible to grow up having had the benefit of participating in a fellowship or family of people who believe in and seek to live by the story of Jesus.

5.10   The 1945 report *Towards the Conversion of England,* in its section on children's evangelism, spoke of the possibility of people holding through life a 'lasting impression' from their childhood encounters with the gospel. It suggested that 'a sudden conversion in later years can be traced to a remembered appeal in childhood'.[3] The sort of evangelism that makes sense with children who may lack parental encouragement is that which will plant lasting impressions even if it does not yield immediate returns. Perhaps too much stress has been placed upon whether there are 'bottoms on pews' to show for our work. It can surely be a matter of considerable – perhaps eternal – significance for a young adult to face the future carrying deep, positive and lasting memories of the Christian community and the story that is believed and lived out by that community. It is to give children the same components that can be found in a Christian home.

SUNDAYS OR MIDWEEK?

5.11   In this experience of the Christian community telling and living its story, the ideal – as was set out in *Children in the Way* – is for such children to be involved in an all-age worship and learning experience Sunday by Sunday. However, this could pose real problems for children with non-attending parents. The family might have other plans on Sunday which involve the children. Children coming without adult support might well feel left out or second-class citizens. Older children in the immediate pre-teen years can feel a little too grown up for some child-related activities.

5.12   We are left with the options of separate children's work on the Sunday or the use of a midweek evening or a combination of both. Because of the increasing use of Sundays for recreational activities in the community and because hardworking, double-income parents are likely to want to get out with their children on Sundays, it is increasingly obvious that midweek, club-type formats would seem to have considerable advantages. While it is true that some churches in some areas still seem to exercise an effective outreach through Sunday activities, it is also noticeable that many churches are beginning to experiment with the weekday option.

Timing can vary. With both parents at work it could well be that the immediate after-school hours are more suitable than time later in the evening. Such clubs could also be providing parents with something of much needed practical help which might, in return, encourage a positive attitude towards the church.

This tie-in between gentle children's evangelism and meeting the needs of the parents might well be part of a wider ministry where churches with their large premises and access to voluntary help (including often a high number of ex-teachers and nurses) could offer child care facilities perhaps, even, financed by local industry.

EXPERIENCING THE CHRISTIAN COMMUNITY

5.13   If the children are to experience the Christian community in a midweek context, however, this says something about the desirable ratio of adults to children. Single leaders, or a very small team of leaders, will hardly convey an experience of the Christian fellowship. Midweek activities, therefore, are likely to be costly in terms of adult time, but churches need to count such costs and recognise the high priority of this work. Ideally there should be men and women in the leadership team. A cross-section of ages is also valuable. Children often warm to and trust older 'grandparent' types of people more than those who are contemporaries of their parents. In addition, the involvement of older people on the team displays an important 'sign' about the place of the elderly in the kingdom. In seeking a high ratio of adults to children the Working Party would also want to draw attention to the need for the most careful scrutiny in regard to any adults who might be asked to work with children.

5.14   A weekday 'club' atmosphere will obviously not be conducive to a traditional worship and teaching approach. This can have real advantages. If the main offering of the church to the child is the Sunday programme, children can form ideas of Christianity being in a compartment distinct from 'real life'. *To share with Christian adults in play and other recreational activities can help children to learn that God is the Lord of all life.* Many practical activities can demonstrate Christian caring such as teaching how to ride a bicycle safely, sports coaching, and not least, helping with homework. (Some 'Black-led' churches have turned to this with a view to helping their children fight against educational disadvantage.)

5.15   Any discussion of the possibility of club and activity centred work must acknowledge the excellent work done by many uniformed organisations who have worked faithfully in this field for decades. The continuous need of such organisations is for more leaders who will commit themselves to the vision and the time needed for such ministry. Churches with church based uniformed groups often slip into an attitude that these organisations have their own supply of potential leaders. *The truth is that the effectiveness in mission of such groups is directly related to the commitment of members of the congregation.* A congregation cannot complain that the children in uniformed movements do not fully identify with the church if the church does not identify with the uniformed movement by providing leadership that demonstrates the underlying unity of movement and congregation.

TELLING THE CHRISTIAN STORY

5.16   In club-like settings the telling of the Christian story will require considerable skill and imagination. 'Epilogues' in youth and children's work can so easily be dull and boring compared to the fun and enjoyment of the rest of the proceedings. They can also convey the impression that we are rather ashamed of our 'Christian bit' and relegate it to a 'hole in the corner'. Our aim should be that our talk of Christ comes out of and relates to the way we live – even when we are 'letting our hair down'.

Diocesan education departments and national voluntary agencies can play a valuable part in training leaders and providing imaginative resources for this kind of ministry. Video material is likely to be increasingly useful and dioceses (or even deaneries) might well need to build up video libraries.

There is a need for high-quality, illustrated take-home material to reinforce the message. This would have the additional value of being accessible to other members of the family. Publishers, denominational central organisations and voluntary agencies could play a valuable role in producing such resources.

5.17 Music is important to most children and can play a vital part in evangelistic work. Songs from other parts of the world Church can be fun to sing, as are many contemporary choruses. There is a need for more of these contemporary songs to be written specially for use with children. There are particular images and levels of emotional intensity in some choruses that make them more suitable for adults (for whom they were originally written) than for children. Restraint and discernment are needed in the choice of and leading of choruses.

5.18 The most valuable ministry to children, however, is at personal level. In a discussion on the problems of communicating with children, especially against the high quality and sophistication of television, one children's worker said:

> But where we win hands down is that we are physically there, by the side of the child. We can show friendship, care, love and interest.

Another children's work leader said:

> I was converted to Jesus at a beach mission when I saw Christianity walking along in jeans.

It is dangerously easy to treat a large number of children as an 'audience'. The ideal is a high ratio of leaders to children and a continuous living out and discussion of the story of Jesus. This will make more impact than an unremitting diet of up-front proclamation. *In a sense we are trying to re-create the ways we communicate within a Christian home at its best.*

5.19 The gospel has to be related to the experience and horizons of children. What is the Good News for children? An experienced children's evangelist told the Working Party that, in his experience, children could grasp the following concepts.

1. A loving heavenly Father (even if there have been bad experiences of earthly fathers).
2. Being a friend of Jesus.
3. Forgiveness.
4. Doing what Jesus says makes for a better way of life.
5. The crucifixion – children can understand heroism and even substitution. The widespread knowledge of Aslan stories has helped many unchurched children to grasp concepts helpful to sharing the gospel story.

5.20   There is an obvious deficiency in a children's ministry focused entirely upon weekdays. The children will not experience the local congregation at worship. Special efforts could be made to draw in the club children and their *parents* at major festivals, and perhaps with a link through to a monthly 'Family Service'. Some might feel that for such children to experience the local congregation at worship would *not* be a helpful experience, and this might well be true. However, should this be the case, the congregation should consider itself and its worship under judgement. The Spirit of Christ must be a Spirit that welcomes and holds the interest of children, for Jesus succeeded in these areas.

5.21   Children need variety – they are easily bored. Not only does there need to be a variety within the weekly programme of activities of the main children's outreach activity – there needs to be a variety of different formats in the course of a year.

The well-worn idea of annual or occasional outings can still prove a bonus to regular work.

An increasing number of churches are finding holiday missions or holiday clubs draw in new members. The experience of many with such holiday projects is that it is often difficult to channel the holiday attenders on into the regular children's work of the church. This is another reason why the week-night club approach may prove a better strategy than a Sunday related activity. Indeed, it may well be that a holiday club might prove the ideal launch pad for a new week-night club. (Should this strategy be pursued, it is important that there is a high level of continuity between the leadership of the holiday project and that of the weekly club.)

In the matter of variety of approach, the uniformed movements with their blend of club nights, Bible class, camps, national and district events with other groups have much to offer in the matter of maintaining interest.

THE APPROPRIATE RESPONSE

5.22   In this attempt to describe the elements that would make for an evangelism appropriate to unchurched childen, we must ask: *what is the appropriate response?* Some might feel critical of what is being described in this report because it does not seem to place much emphasis upon guaranteeing future membership. Some might ask, 'How in this chummy and cheery activity with children are we going to make repentance and faith happen?'

Some words from Dr John Stott might be apposite:

> To 'evangelise' in the New Testament usage does not mean to win converts, as it usually does when we use the word. Evangelism is the announcement of the Good News, irrespective of the results.[4]

5.23 Westerhoff in his analysis of faith development argues that the most likely period of life when conversion takes place is in late adolescence or in early childhood. However, he stresses an important point:

> Conversion ... is never an isolated event devoid of all elements of nurture. Nurture and conversion are a unified whole.[5]

5.24 Sensitivity and the proper concern that children should not be manipulated does not mean, however, that children cannot and do not make clear-cut steps forward in their personal faith journeys. Some can come under a very real sense of conviction. Some develop a remarkable sense of the presence of the Lord. But all of this should be left to the promptings of the Holy Spirit. Workers amongst children must answer truthfully when children seek advice about responses they wish to make. Where care must be taken is in the matter of putting children under pressure to make particular types of response. The main task of children's evangelism, however, is for children to experience what it is like to live in fellowship with Christians and to learn about the Christ upon whom those Christians centre their lives.

5.25 Francis Bridger, in his valuable book *Children Finding Faith* has a helpful section where he applies Westerhoff's thinking to interpret the responses and apparent 'decisions' that children may make to the gospel:

> What, then, are we doing when we preach the gospel to children? I think on Westerhoff's logic we are doing several things that might best be described as pre-conversional. Firstly, we are *sowing seed for the future*. Children who hear the gospel may not yet be ready for the act of surrender and the stage of owned faith but they can store away the truth for the time when it will become relevant...
>
> Secondly, we may be *persuading a child simply to switch his affiliation*... It is unlikely, given what we know about the structure of child development, that a junior child who comes along to a mission or Sunday school will be converted in the adult sense of making an independent decision to reorientate his life. What is much more likely is that the child who appears to make a

decision for Christ at a mission, club or Sunday school has decided to start a new affiliation ... the desire to give his loyalty to a new group (the mission, church or whatever) can represent a genuinely heart-felt act... It represents a powerful act of commitment.

But the meaning of such a commitment may lie in affiliation to the complex of persons and beliefs which make up the group, rather than to a personal acceptance of a set of truths... We should not be looking for responses which are characteristically adult but for those which are realistically appropriate to child development.[6]

5.26 There is, however, one particular response that every children's evangelist should wish for and *that is that children should want to pray.* There is abundant evidence that many people have learned simple, trusting prayer in their childhood years and have never lost the practice. Part of the corporate life of the children's club, service or camp should be expressing thanks to God for the blessings of life, and praying for 'ordinary' matters as well as special needs. Children should be asked to suggest topics for prayer and praise. They need to develop a practical understanding that their heavenly Father wants us to share our joys and anxieties with him. *Prayer is evidence of repentance and faith.* It is a recognition of the need to turn to God as opposed to others, and an expression of trust. Children can be taught to regard God as a loving Father to whom they can talk naturally. Very often the naturalness of children's prayers, and the faith they reveal, can minister to their adult leaders!

5.27 Throughout this chapter we have discussed how adults can exercise a ministry among children. Those who engage in such ministry would want to insist on inserting a corrective point – much of the evangelism among children is effected by the infectious faith and enthusiasm of other children. Many churches report that the best recruiting is done by the children themselves. For children to be able to do this, they have to have a situation to which they can invite their friends where they will not be embarrassed. If children come to a service, club, holiday project or mission once or twice and then never again it is not enough to say 'they were not really interested'. We must ask ourselves – *why?*

6 Evangelism in the Classroom?

If I was to offer through a Missionary Society to teach my subject to children who want to learn in a Ugandan school, I would be called a 'Missionary'. I would be sent on my way with a Valedictory Service and adopted by a church who would remember me. Because I am teaching my subject in a nearby State school, nobody seems to think I need prayer. Yet I could be dealing with many difficult children who don't appear to want to learn anything. (Surrey school teacher)

6.1   If it is true that, at present, the churches in the country are drawing in no more than 15 per cent of the child population, it is also true that the schools draw in virtually all. Whether they like it or not, children have to go to school. This being so, should not the churches develop a strategy for evangelism in schools?

6.2   The Church of England has a long and honourable history of involvement in education focusing particularly on Church schools and Colleges of Education.

In many parishes good relationships exist between county schools and the local churches, and clergy are welcomed into classroom and staff room with the agreement of the headteacher.

EDUCATION ACTS

6.3   In addition to long-standing and good relationships between Church and school, there is the fact of legal requirement in the case of Religious Education (RE). The 1944 Education Act made the teaching of Religious Education compulsory – a status granted to no other subject. The 1944 term was, in fact, 'Religious Instruction' (RI) rather than 'Religious Education' which perhaps conveys something of the mood of the time. Schools were also required to begin each day with an act of worship. The Act and its requirements reflected the mood of the public in such matters. As we have seen in Chapter 1, the vast majority of children at that time attended a Sunday school, presumably with parental encouragement.

The religious education envisaged in 1944 was essentially a teaching of the Bible set against the background assumption that Christianity was built into the cultural, moral and spiritual fabric of the nation. Because of this, and because the Church had such a heavy investment in schools, Church and State were effectively working in partnership.

6.4   In 1988 the Education Reform Act came onto the statute book and in the intervening 44 years the schools had worked their way through dramatic social, cultural and religious changes. No longer were the majority of children coming from homes that supported the Sunday school. The 1960s saw a questioning and often a rejection of many of the authoritarian and 'respected' elements of British life and the Church was amongst the areas affected. In addition to such a drop in public esteem, there was a considerable amount of rethinking about the appropriate ways to teach religious subjects with consequential moves away from content transmission towards the encouragement of experience and discovery. This changed the way that the Bible was handled in the classroom.

6.5   Perhaps the biggest upheaval was the development of this country from one in which religious and ethnic minorities were numerically tiny to one in which they became undeniably significant. Immigration brought large numbers of Muslims, Hindus and Sikhs into Britain (alongside many West Indian Christians). While their overall numbers are small – some 4 per cent of the total population – their concentration within particular communities is sometimes high. Several Local Education Authorities and many headteachers have had to face the fact that large numbers on the school rolls (sometimes the majority of pupils) have a strong commitment to a religion other than Christianity.

This change in the complexion of some communities took place at the same time as the changing thought about religious education away from a 'confessional' approach towards a more generalised study of religion. Such a study implied no adherence or initial commitment to any particular religion and recognised that children were now well aware of the existence of many faiths. It was considered no longer appropriate to teach RE with reference to Christianity alone.

6.6   Those parts of the 1988 Education Act that relate to the place of religion in the curriculum and in school life are in part a reflection of the changes since 1944 and in part a reaction to those changes. While not pretending that the national mood regarding Christianity is the same as that 40 years ago, there is an attempt to reaffirm that RE must be taught against the understanding that the main religious tradition of this country is Christianity, while not forgetting that other religious traditions are now part of the national complexion. The daily 'collective act of worship' was to be 'wholly or mainly of a broadly Christian character' avoiding on the one hand a blurring of distinctive faiths but also avoiding indoctrination or sectarianism on the other.

6.7   At first sight the 1988 Act appears greatly to strengthen the place for communicating Christianity within the life of the school. A number of important qualifications, however, need to be kept in mind.

While the Act underlines the primary place of Christianity in the teaching of RE, the fact of the matter in a significant minority of schools is that children of other faiths and cultures are present in large numbers. This problem is even present in Church schools because, for example, some Muslim families would rather send their children to a school where God is respected than to one which they regard as totally secular. To expect teachers, in some way, to proselytise is unthinkable. Parents of other faiths can always avail themselves of the provision that children can be withdrawn from RE lessons and even receive teaching in their own faith by an appropriate person; but within a school community such withdrawals could be emotionally uncomfortable for the children.

A 'School Assembly' is not necessarily an 'act of worship'. In his book *Worship, Worries and Winners*[1] Terence Copley points out that the essential ingredient in people coming together for worship is their holding of common values. A school, unless it is a Church school (and even here one would add provisos), is not a religious community with its members bound together by a common view of life, or of God, or of themselves as a worshipping group. As we have seen, some schools contain worshipping members of faiths other than Christianity. Further, there may well be children present whose parents are consciously agnostic, atheistic or secular humanists.

The renewed insistence upon a daily Act of Collective Worship poses genuine problems for those who carry the responsibility for making the necessary arrangements. In recent years daily assemblies have disappeared

in many schools. Sometimes there has been a weekly assembly, sometimes occasional assemblies for different sections of the school. The new
demands of the Act have therefore necessitated quite major changes in the
daily timetable. Further, many schools simply do not have the space to
assemble all the pupils in one place at one time. Compliance with the
Act, therefore, calls for more than one assembly every day and this at a
time when the new Basic Curriculum requires more time in the classroom. It also needs to be remembered that staff are at liberty to choose
not to attend the act of worship.

While RE is in the new Act as part of the Basic Curriculum which
promotes the spiritual, moral, cultural, mental and physical development
of pupils, it is *not* a core subject and no national attainment targets or
assessment criteria were proposed as for other subjects. While moves are
afoot to suggest targets and criteria at Local Education Authority level
some RE teachers fear that it will still not have the place in most schools
that is envisaged in the new Act.

OPPORTUNITIES

6.8   While the new Act may not have taken matters back to the situation of the 1940s (which would have been impossible, in any case) it
contains much to encourage Christians. It affirms the importance of
'Christian belief'. It emphasises the place of 'spiritual development'. It
recognises the need for information *plus experience*. It is clear that the requirement for a daily Act of Worship is opening up a host of opportunities for church people, both clergy and lay, to go into schools and
help hard-pressed headteachers. These opportunities must not be missed,
but they require sensitive and skilled handling.

6.9   Does this mean that evangelism is possible in school premises and in
school time?

If, by evangelism, we mean an attempt to win converts, the answer
must be 'no'. That would be to abuse the provisions of the Act.

If, by evangelism, we mean what has been described in the previous
chapter – giving children an experience of 'affiliative faith' – the answer
again has to be in the negative. It is simply impossible to create and maintain the conditions for this to happen. Some Church schools, however,
may in their effects go some way towards achieving this end. The

National Society in its 1984 publications *A Future in Partnership*, sets out
ten characteristics of a Church school. The first of these reads: '*A safe
place* where there is no ideological pressure and yet Christian influences
are built into the ethos and teaching as signals for children to detect.' The
fifth characteristic is described as '*a house of the gospel* in which, starting at
governor and staff level, there is a deliberate attempt to link the concerns
of Christ's gospel with the life of the school, and to do this in educational terms'.[2]

If, by evangelism, we mean allowing children to encounter the content
of the gospel and to learn something of its implications in the lives of
people and communities, then there is every chance that this can happen.
It will need to happen, however, *in the context of education rather than mission*.

6.10   Invitations to go into schools to take assemblies or to engage in
classroom activity are chances not to be missed, but those receiving them
need to be sensitive to the authority and wishes of the headteacher and
they require a particular range of gifts and skills. No good purpose is
served by boring children in the name of Christ and his Church. Those
who receive invitations would do well to seek out all such help that is
available. One organisation, for example, offers the following eight
admonitions:

1.   Work closely with the school. Before beginning to prepare, check
     that you know the age range of the children, who else will be pre-
     sent, and the amount of time you are allowed. It will be helpful to
     know in advance of any children from non-Christian religious
     backgrounds who will be there. Will there be parents present?
2.   Let the school know in advance what your theme will be.
3.   Stick closely to the rules you have been given by the school.
     Above all NEVER OVERRUN YOUR TIME.
4.   Do not try to do too much – make just one or two points.
5.   The average modern child has little or no Bible or Church
     knowledge.
6.   Prepare carefully and use a variety of methods – drama, modern
     songs, music.
7.   Avoid direct evangelism. It is completely unacceptable in a county
     school.

8.   Do not ask or expect the children to join in Christian prayers or songs. Check with the school beforehand whether it is acceptable for you to give them the chance of participation. [3]

Several dioceses issue guidelines for leading Acts of Worship as do the National Society and a number of other agencies. [4]

CLERGY TRAINING

6.11   It is clear that parish clergy are extremely likely in the course of their ministry to find themselves invited into schools. The Working Party, in the light of this, asked a number of theological colleges to describe what preparation they offered students in this field. It is well known that the colleges in our present system have a thankless task in trying to meet so many competing requirements and expectations. Nevertheless, it has to be reported that the picture which emerged from our inquiries revealed no overall philosophy, little recognition of the significance of schools' work and very inadequate theoretical or practical provision. In this we concur with the recent finding of the Archbishops' Commission on Rural Areas. [5] An obvious resource to the colleges (and courses) in this matter ought to be the local diocesan education staff.

6.12   There is an understandable view of theological education which holds that initial training should concentrate on theology and spirituality to encourage the right sort of thinking, while practice is best learned on the job under 'training vicars' augmented by post-ordination training and, later, continuing ministerial education. However, all too often, assistant curates find themselves thrown into the practicalities of their work from day one in the parish, therefore there is a need for an overview covering college and diocese to ensure that the right skills are taught at the right time.

VOLUNTARY ACTIVITY IN SCHOOLS

6.13   Because schools are communities as well as places of learning, they have always tended to encourage the development of voluntary groupings. This has led to the formation of many Christian activities in lunch times and in after school hours. Many are inspired and run by teachers on school staffs, some by pupils themselves, some drawing in parents and others drawing on clergy or neighbourhood full-time Christian youth or schools' workers. The Working Party were reminded of the very wide range of such activities. At the very least they stimulate the witness of the Christian children who attend, but it is also highly likely that they have a positive effect upon many children who, at present, are rarely seen inside a church building. Some Christian agencies employ specialist schools' workers to resource such voluntary activities and these have to learn the sensitivities and boundaries that must control their work.

The churches need to remember that one tactless episode from an inexperienced or over-enthusiastic individual could set back the patient and continuing work in the school by others either on the teaching staff or who have access in a voluntary capacity.

COMMUNITY INVOLVEMENT

6.14   One of the objectives of the 1988 Act was to encourage greater involvement of parents in the organisation of the schools their children attend. It is important that Christian parents, therefore, should not be so busy in 'church activities' that they have no time to be involved in the school. Parents, often through the Parent Teacher Association, or Friends Association, can give practical help with maintenance of buildings and equipment and the provision of library books. They can become involved in the social and fundraising activities of the school. They can offer assistance on school trips or regular visits to swimming pools or sports fields. They can often find themselves welcomed into classroom activities. As already noted, they become involved in the out-of-schools clubs – and not only those with a Christian agenda. Not least, they can involve themselves in prayer support groups. Many head-teachers are grateful for and encouraged by the presence of such groups.

Community relationships, of course, are a two-way process. Schools can often offer unique contributions to a supportive local community and nearby church. School choirs and orchestras, for instance, could breathe life into many a church festival service.

6.15   Parents (and others in local churches) can also play a valuable part in the life of schools by serving as governors. The more bridges created between schools and the local community and its churches, the better. Governors have the responsibility of determining aims, objectives and general policy in the life and work of the school. As well as working towards educational excellence each school needs to have its own distinct 'humanness' and spiritual ethos – these qualities matter to parents. One of the stated aims in the 1988 Act is the 'spiritual development' of the pupils. Obviously there are particular areas of expertise that governors need to develop but resources are available from several quarters.[6]

TEACHERS

6.16   Teaching has always been a demanding profession and the present situation has brought extra demands and pressures. Churches need to remember that those teachers in their congregations are not excluded from the pressures and the sense of being undervalued which affect many in the profession.

6.17   Christian teachers need our prayers and encouragement. They must not carry the burden of false expectations. Their task is to be good, highly professional teachers rather than evangelists. The (somewhat non-inclusive) words of the 1970 Durham Report are still apposite:

> To press for acceptance of a particular faith or belief system is the duty and privilege of the Churches and other similar religious bodies. It is certainly not the task of a teacher in a county school. If the teacher is to press for any conversion, it is conversion from a shallow and unreflective attitude to life. If he is to press for commitment, it is commitment to the religious quest, to that search for meaning, purpose and value which is open to all men.[7]

6.18   This professionalism, however, does not rule out the natural witness of a Christian character. If Christians in the teaching profession seek to live and work in the light of the gospel, there can be little doubt that such a light will be seen by others. At a time when many are reported to be leaving the teaching profession, we need to encourage more Christians to view this work as a vocation with deep significance for the life and health of our society.

6.19   But teachers are not the only Christians in schools. In many ways the most effective living and sharing of the gospel is that which takes place amongst the children themselves and they, with all their natural enthusiasm, often exercise the most effective ministry of all.

7   Building New Bridges

The opportunity to touch, even marginally, those non-churchgoers who sent their children to Sunday school on a Sunday has gone and has not been replaced. But if we are to reach our children – and many parents appreciate the value of religious education – we need to form new bridges. (*Christian England* (MARC Europe, 1991), p. 103.)

7.1   The Working Party advertised widely in the Church press, requesting details of activities, events and schemes that have proved successful in reaching children outside the normal life of the Church. While grateful for the many replies received, it has been difficult to select a few from the large number of detailed, enthusiastic responses and highlight them.

7.2   What follows is not a blueprint for success, but rather a few headings, with glimpses of what others have done that may stimulate local church communities to develop ideas of their own which relate to their situation and to the resources they have available. *Children in the Way* states:

> Every parish will have its own strengths and weaknesses with which to work, and the needs of a particular community will suggest different priorities.

AIMS

7.3   The work undertaken does seem to fall into some easily-defined groups. Nearly all testify to the need to identify clear aims. One Southampton parish puts it like this:

> Our aims, with adults and children alike, are to let people know that the church is there, and to make contacts with the church as positive an experience as possible. To this end clergy and laity are involved in local schools and youth organisations, and we have various events through the year which attract a wider group of children than just those who attend our youth organisations.

66

The parish of Braintree in Essex says:

> Our aim in establishing the JAM Club was primarily (i) to give children a basic knowledge of simple truths about God and Jesus so that they would grow up with some background knowledge of Christianity; and (ii) to communicate these truths in a setting that was fun and enjoyable and in a caring relationship with the leaders. We wanted them to understand from experience that God loves and cares about them – many from broken homes don't know much about love at first-hand. The approachability and caring of the leaders may teach them this even if they don't take in much of the actual 'teaching'.
>
> A secondary aim has also been to reach out to the families of the children; and to this end parents are invited to different events and the leaders make every effort to get to know the parents. But this is a slow process, and I'm afraid there is not a lot of result to show for it – apart from a friendly smile from a mum in the street.
>
> Our aim has not been to evangelise the children directly but to lay foundations; though, of course, we encourage them to move on to older groups in the church when they leave JAM Club and include them in invitations to any outreach event in the church.

MID-WEEK CLUBS

7.4   One fertile area for development seems to be the mid-week club, often taking place immediately after school. Three of the most significant responses received fell into this category and they are all worth quoting at some length. The 'Cats Club' at Brighouse in West Yorkshire started as a successor to the 'Adventurers' (a USPG sponsored club). The parish priest describes it thus:

> It was decided to run a club for all children in the parish, not just those of church families (for which Adventurers had largely catered). The club would aim to teach the Christian faith in a relaxed and informal atmosphere, with games and refreshments as well as teaching and worship. It would be run by a team of 8-10 adults from the congregation, including some men, to ensure that we attracted boys as well as girls. We decided on the name Cats Club – Cats being short for Catechumens and Catechism. We obtained the support of the three junior schools in our parish, and through them sent out a leaflet and an invitation to all children in the parish, except those who were already committed to other churches in the area.
>
> Over the past four years, the Cats Club has become the major evangelistic thrust in this parish. It brings together over 50 children every Thursday

evening, all of whom come from families who have no other church connection – at least, to begin with! The age range is the junior one – 7-11.
Meetings begin with organised games, followed by worship, followed by a
lesson and activity – it might be music, drama, modelling, art work and so
on. The last ten minutes are spent having orange juice and biscuits, chatting
informally with the children, meeting parents as they come to collect them
etc.

The Cats Club plays a major part in the Family Eucharist on the first Sunday of each month. The Eucharist is shortened and 'informalised', children
lead singing, prayers, do dramatised versions of the Gospel, etc. A good proportion of parents come to support them, and this has led to some of them
becoming part of the life of the church.

When a major saint's day or red-letter day falls on a Thursday, the Cats
Club puts on a children's Eucharist as part of its meeting. Many parents and
friends support this and it provides a good teaching vehicle for both children
and parents. In the last year of their membership, children are encouraged to
join the junior Confirmation class. This meets at the same time as Cats and is
indeed an integral part of it. All the children support the candidates on the
Confirmation day.

Another Yorkshire parish priest wrote in with his account:

Apart from a regular Sunday morning Explorer group (7-11 years) of 25-30
meeting in the church halls after 10 minutes of the main church service, we
have an annual children's outreach [summer holiday club] and a club night
fortnightly on Fridays.

Explorers meet every Sunday except on the monthly family service; over
one-third of the children are from non-church families and come with friends
or as a result of the summer club or club night.

In an effort to get to know the children better I started a club night. This
is mainly fun and good fellowship – games, crafts and outings. It is open to
any 7-11-year-old; on average 20-30 with over 50 on the books. We are going to have a barbecue for the families after this summer's outreach, as it is
obviously best to have whole families.

At Braintree in Essex the club has successfully attracted many children
who previously had no contact with the church:

We set up a mid-week children's club at our church with the main aim of
reaching children who would not normally come to Sunday school. The club
is called JAM Club ('Jesus and Me' Club) and is for children age 5-10.

At first the children who attended were about 50 per cent church
members. Now the group is predominantly children with no church
background, most of whom come from the local area which is mainly council

housing. Most of these children have little knowledge of even the most basic stories about Jesus – to some of them he is only a swear word.

The club meets on Tuesdays from 4.30-5.45 pm. This time incorporates Bible teaching in groups, craft work, games, singing, outings, activities etc. in varying combinations. 'Bible teaching' is very informal with some practical involvement or discussion with the children. Between 20-40 minutes is spent on this, varying according to the material involved and other activities planned.

Another important aspect of the club is working for awards. Again this is geared at a very simple level with small awards at regular intervals and very easily obtained. In this way no child loses out from lack of ability.

We always have a drink and biscuits too – very important!

All Saints, Ilkley, is another parish that have found a weekday slot after school to be most helpful:

The Explorers Club (7-10s) starts straight after school on a Friday, when the leaders collect the children from the school and walk them across to the church hall. Here they have squash and a biscuit, then some active games related to the theme, then three-quarters of an hour's teaching (some together, some in groups). Of the 52 children, 48 come from non-church families, whose parents appreciate an extra hour of freedom!

HOLIDAY CLUBS

7.5 The Young Families Department of the Mothers' Union contributed enormously to our research. The Working Party wish to pay a special tribute to the MU and to the tremendous voluntary work they are doing through their publications, and with children around the country. Many of our examples came from parishes supported and helped by the Mothers' Union, and this was especially true of a large number of holiday clubs of varying kinds. A common pattern emerged. They were largely organised to last from two days to two weeks of the school holidays, and were intended for any children who cared to come.

The general trend seems to be that church children form some 40-50 per cent of the membership of such clubs. Often there is follow-up work and contact is made at Christmas with a card or a visit. Most such clubs are run for children under 11 years. Several parishes spoke of the value of outreach to children who need such activities because of a lack of parental presence or support. A number of these clubs give churches an opportunity to work ecumenically.

Holy Week activities for young people at St Mary the Virgin, Calne are typical of such events in many parishes:

Notices and posters were put out before the event in shops and schools. Children were asked to pay a nominal subscription each day. They met at 10 am for a welcome and the singing of a theme song. A video followed and then children subdivided into age groups for follow-up work. An hour or so of workshops followed, during which refreshments were served. Finally the children gathered together for some songs, a recap. of the story, prizes, notices and short prayers. This year the parish extended the club to include some special activities and a service on Good Friday.

A rural West Midlands parish wrote to tell us of a summer holiday club:

The parish church organised a Holiday Club for the children of the village over three days towards the end of the summer holidays. There was a lot of hard work and preparation involved by the leaders, but it was a real outreach to the children and the numbers increased daily as they brought their friends along.

We started with a short time in church where we sang choruses. We had a short Bible story, and then the children were given the opportunity to choose which group they would like to join – music, drama, craft, cookery, kite making, etc. Packed lunches were brought and then in the afternoon outdoor activities were also on offer – nature walks, games, rambles.

It gave us the chance to speak to children and get to know those who might not usually come to church. We also kept records of the children who came and tried to follow up with a visit and Christmas card to as many as possible.

Scripture Union organises many excellent holiday clubs and publishes useful resource material for leaders.

OTHER PROJECTS

7.6   Specific projects depend very much on local needs and opportunities but can be very valuable.

Two people in a rural Devon parish persuaded the local PCC to let the young people from local villages decorate and use the parish hall. It is now the King's Coffee Bar. The age range is 9-14 and it is 'the first step that these children would have made towards the Church'. The obvious lesson is that the majority of young people are not where the Church thinks they are, nor will the young people accept where the Church is. Evangelism involves the Church moving out to where young people are.

EVENTS

7.7   Occasional or regular events have their place and can be run on a parish, a village or a deanery basis. The Modbury Deanery in Exeter diocese runs an annual deanery camp. Sunday school children bring their friends and, sometimes, their parents.

A Southampton parish's junior church held a sports evening one May:

> This was organised by the junior church leaders and supported by the clergy and other members of the congregation. What little finance was involved came from junior church funds. The aim was to have an enjoyable evening, and to let children know that the junior church was there. I suppose that this is 'pre-evangelistic', but it is similar to the sort of work we do with many adults. Some of the children who came did then maintain some connection with the junior church, but we have not had a lot of success in integrating them into mainstream church life.

Erith deanery in Rochester diocese organised a Children's Council Fun Day:

> 3-7-year-olds were accepted when accompanied by responsible adults. 7-11-year-olds were the main focus of the day. Over 11s acted as helpers. We believe that all the activities were evangelistic, as we mixed with and talked to boys and girls, parents and leaders. The day culminated in a short open-air act of worship.

Some events were linked to festivals. One unusual example came to us from Chapel Allerton in Leeds:

> A Pancake Party was organised, financed by the PCC and run by junior church leaders, which ran on later into a Maundy Thursday and a Good Friday event. One parent later wrote in the parish magazine: 'It was a wonderfully happy occasion with games, filmstrip, songs, prayers – and pancakes! To see so many children gathered there, and so many new faces was a delight. What an excellent way to share the joy of Christ and illustrate the warmth of the Church family.'

The report of the Archbishops' Commission on Rural Areas *Faith in the Countryside* has many examples of work going on around the country:

> A parish church in Cornwall held a Praise Party last October 31st as a positive

alternative to Halloween activities, and this attracted a number of children who might have been out knocking on doors and frightening elderly people.[1]

MISSIONS

7.8   Of course missions as such can also have an impact. Various names were mentioned by correspondents, and it is always worth checking with children's advisers or other experts to see who is available and can be recommended. Voluntary and missionary organisations, religious communities and diocesan education teams are a ready source of help. Regular missions are undertaken by teams from the Church Army, including some excellent beach missions, Scripture Union and other national bodies.

PRE-SCHOOL GROUPS

7.9   One very popular way of providing a service for the community and at the same time enabling Christians to get alongside those with little or no church affiliation is the pre-school group. A correspondent from Prestwick, for example, wrote to tell us of work going on in that part of Scotland:

> I thought you might be interested in the Alpha Kindergarten, which is a pre-school group run in our church hall. This was opened in August 1988 with the aim of reaching out into the community.
> So far we have been very encouraged by the appreciation of parents and support from the local Playgroup Association. Having been quite open about our aims in our introductory leaflet, it gives us great freedom in teaching and praying with/for the children. Information about Guest Services, Sunday school events, etc. can be included in newsletters, thus reaching families who have no church contact.

7.10   There are times when such projects are best organised on a wider base. From the diocese of St Edmundsbury and Ipswich comes this visionary example of real excellence:

> Much of the diocese is very rural. Communities are losing their schools, post offices, etc. Under-fives provision is also rare. In rural areas perhaps the greatest pressure is isolation.
> A conference in 1985 identified the need for mobile family resources in rural areas, where there are few community facilities, and to make information accessible to families with young children.

A family caravan was given to the Family Life Project, and this, with two others, is now being developed by the diocese. They seat about nine people, have toilet, cooking and storage facilities. They are stocked with literature, toys and games.

The caravans tour the villages, parking by the green or the playing field, or in the pub yard. Word soon gets round and people turn up. Even new vicars, finding it hard to cover a multiple benefice, find the caravan a good way of meeting some of their parishioners.

In the summer holidays the caravans reach more lives. Using them as a base, volunteers run play schemes for children up to 14 years. Some schemes run for three afternoons during one week, others for two half-days each week during August. Children come together for crafts, painting, games, sweet-making, kite flying, races, even pony rides. Once again the potential for helping and supporting one another is discovered and put into practice. The remote village finds resources within itself that it had not suspected, and the feeling of isolation recedes just a little.

The Church is meeting children and their families where they are.

SCHOOLS

7.11 The Working Party received a large number of stories about Church/school involvement. As suggested already, this is an area where a great deal of sensitivity needs to be shown; but nonetheless much good work can be achieved. A few ideas illustrate the variety of approaches that can be successfully adopted.

In Exeter, a group of churches including Anglicans, Baptists and several other Free Churches appointed a schools' worker. Before bringing this appointment to fruition, they worked hard to develop relationships between schools and churches. They sought to incorporate qualified adults in the programme of school life, particularly in taking assemblies. Assembly outlines were produced, and a conference for local Christian teachers was held. School lunchtime groups for Christian pupils were formed. With the goodwill of the schools, a 'high profile' event was organised every second week using loud music, flashing lights and silly games. On the alternate weeks a small Bible study based programme was introduced for those intrigued by the previous week's event. Every effort was made to ensure that local Christian adults were involved in as many aspects of school life as possible.

In Reading, the local churches produced a directory of local people with an interesting story to tell, who would be available for occasional school visits and assemblies. In Bristol and other dioceses, training sessions have been arranged for people offering their help in schools.

A correspondent from Maidstone wrote:

> I am responsible for regular school visits – infant and junior, in the area. Over four years a good working relationship has grown up with heads of about 25 schools. In two schools we have initiated Christian clubs. We have about 50 children attending 'Supergang' in the lunchtime and 12 attend 'Kingsquad' after school. They are both run as any other school club, and the majority of the children have no connections with any church.

In Ipswich there are 17 different churches represented on the executive committee for Christian Youth Ministries. The CYM team have had invitations into all the senior schools, and many of the primary schools in the area, through which they encourage school groups. This team is a member of the Scripture Union Link-Up scheme, which gives leaders of school groups personal contact with an experienced SU worker, who can offer training, advice, resources and links with other schools in the area.

7.12   More locally various efforts are being made successfully. In Forest Hall, Newcastle, the parish church actively encourages lunchtime meetings in school run by young people from the church, and lunchtime clubs in two local primary schools.

The Christian community at Sparkbrook, Birmingham set up:

> termly 'School Weeks' with an ecumenical team to take a series of assemblies and lessons on mainly festival themes. Drama, music, puppets, sketchboard, songs are all used in seeking to communicate well. We are seeking also to network the schools with Christian churches or groups taking a prayerful/visiting/serving responsibility for the schools (of all kinds) in their area. So far we have regular access to about 14 primary schools and 3 secondary schools.

7.13   Some ideas are novel and inspired. The local church in Knutsford, Cheshire, offers Christian books to school libraries. The church bookstall manager was received enthusiastically when he took a bookstall to one of the local primary schools.

Others are well-tried and tested, but still exceedingly effective. At Basingstoke, a local Christian wrote:

> Our Team Vicar is school governor at our parish school. There are visits to the church, and he visits school regularly and knows the staff, children and parents. He and his wife are members of a local baby-sitting circle, and have contact with local families.

SPIRITUALITY – AND THE USE OF CHURCHES AND CATHEDRALS WITH CHILDREN

7.14 It must be remembered that faith and Church are not always linked. *Children in the Way* states:

> There is some evidence that, while young people generally are not convinced about the place and importance of the Church, they are searching for a faith and for spirituality.[2]

Many churches are finding that children from different backgrounds and experiences respond to opportunities to explore and deepen their spirituality. Workshops in cathedrals, churches and elsewhere have had enthusiastic and often moving responses, when children have been encouraged to learn something about the use of silence and meditation, to respond to their feelings of awe and wonder, to express their deepest thoughts and emotions in art and craft, music and drama.

During the past ten years this work has been developing in many ways as people have been encouraged to look at the much under-used resources in the Church, the church buildings and cathedrals, and to use them in exciting, educational and experimental ways. It is often in such work in a church or cathedral, as they touch stone, contemplate the light coming through stained glass, are encouraged to enter into the vision of the builders by drama, listen to music, explore symbols, discover the wonder of silence and much else, that children have deep spiritual experiences that often lead them to deeper questioning and thought about life and about the Christian understanding of it.

In answer to demands from schools and parishes the diocese of Salisbury, for example, appointed Michael Beesley as an Advisory Teacher working full-time in schools helping teachers and pupils develop their spirituality, and especially their use of stilling and silence. Similar work is being done by diocesan advisers who have been encouraged by the work of the Alistair Hardy Research Project and that of David Hay.

THE USE OF BUILDINGS

7.15 The use of cathedrals and churches for days and events is growing, and many dioceses now have regular times when children are gathered for such possibilities as are mentioned in the previous paragraph. The diocese of Bristol was a pioneer in these activities, and similar opportunities are offered in Bath and Wells, Exeter, Salisbury, Canterbury, Lichfield,

Norwich, St Albans, Coventry, Gloucester, Ely, Birmingham, Durham and elsewhere. Many cathedrals have also established education centres for daily work with children, using a variety of approaches and methods. The Pilgrim Association is one organisation that links those working in this field for annual study and development, and for the sharing of ideas.

Parish churches too are places of rich resources for the children of a locality to be enabled to be enriched and to grow in their spiritual life and their understanding of the Christian faith. Many resources are available to use in such work, including a detailed and imaginative set of cards by Dorothy Jamal, published by CEM.

Educational visits are not often regarded as a possible place for evangelism. Yet the people whom children meet when they visit places of worship often remain fixed in the children's minds as examples of Christians. What do children see when they visit your church? What does the building say to them about God and his people? What do the posters, the state of the building, whether the door is open or closed say to those who visit for whatever reason?

It is a valuable exercise for the PCC and other church members to look at their church as if for the first time and as if a child. They should try to *feel* the atmosphere, *see* the familiar in a new way, and *consider* what message the church is giving to visitors before anyone utters a word.

SUPPORT

7.16   There is always a suspicion that the reason why so many churches fail to make significant moves to children 'on the edge' is a failure to give it sufficient priority. Certainly all such projects require support and help. Mention has already been made of financial help that some projects need from parishes, but money is not everything.

7.17   All these projects are expensive in human terms. Parishes need to free sufficient people from 'in-house' responsibilities to undertake evangelistic roles with children. A Yorkshire parish writes:

> The PCC pays our expenses and we have a pianist and four other committed leaders. The five of us each take a group of children and we explore the faith together using SU teaching materials as a base, with singing, games and activities.

Such people cannot then be expected also to run the church choir, form the backbone of the PCC, or be Enrolling Member of the Mothers' Union!

7.18   The most significant area of support, however, must be that of prayer. The same Yorkshire parish again:

> I have a little group of 'aunties' who pray for the children and the Missionary group pray for special needs and events.

7.19   Further support is often available from national or diocesan sources. Many correspondents testified to the value, for example, of *Together,* a monthly selection of good ideas for work with children, published by the National Society. The Church Pastoral Aid Society, the Mothers' Union, the Bible Society and Scripture Union all produce a wide range of materials. Diocesan Advisers also produce support materials and run training sessions. Most dioceses have resource centres where books, videos, tapes, etc. are available to parishes on loan. *Faith in the Countryside* points to a successful variation on the theme:

> The diocese of St Albans has adapted a caravan as a travelling resource centre, stocked with audio-visual aids, books, tape cassette and video recorder. This is moved from parish to parish, spending a month at each.[3]

Dioceses also have human resources – youth and children's advisers who are usually available to train local leaders, to offer advice and help, and to lead an activity themselves. Religious communities, missionary societies and the Church Army are further rich sources of help. The local community can often be a wonderful place of help, with people and resources of many kinds.

PROBLEMS

7.20   It would be naive to suggest that there are not problems. One deceptively simple sentence from Braintree in Essex highlights this:

> Of course we've learnt from experience and made many mistakes along the way!

Evangelism is by definition reaching out into the unknown. Projects will not always be successful, but even the unsuccessful ones provide learning experience.

7.21   Often the most significant problems arise when attempts are made to link children with whom contact has been made to the local church. If evangelism is to be lasting and effective then such links need to be forged, children need to have contact with the worshipping community. Such links can be difficult:

Sometimes we take a song (once a worship dance) into the church service to help the children feel part of the church family – otherwise there is little in the service that reaches 'non-Anglican' children (those from outside or those who are uncommitted).

Sometimes the problem is a cultural one:

It is hard for ministers to please everyone and we do use the ASB form of service. But a lot of the language in the old prayers, collects and hymns used while the children are in and in the family services is incomprehensible to the average TV educated child; particularly if he comes from a deprived background. (However it does have to be said that many children love poetic language which is not always within their immediate comprehension.)

Sometimes the problem is an organisational one. At one church visited recently the children stayed in church for the first ten minutes before going out to Sunday school, Pathfinders, etc. During their ten minute stay they sang a hymn and made their confession! And in how many churches do the youngsters come in to the Parish Communion during the Offertory hymn? 'We are the Body of Christ', says the celebrant. The congregation shares the Peace. THEN the children come in! Some churches have found that to bring the children in *at* the Peace and to let them share it with the congregation has brought about a new understanding and deeper acceptance of physical contact at this point by all the congregation.

Fortunately the churches are all recognising the need for well-written material that is accessible to young and old alike.

7.22   A further significant problem, however, is the attitude of some of our congregations. The Working Party heard many stories of youngsters coming to faith only to be turned off by the lack of welcome in their local church. We often blame inadequate confirmation preparation for the level of drop-out, but is that really the reason? One letter from a parishioner may illustrate the problem:

If we must have Youth Services, do they have to be at the Eucharist? I had always understood it was a Sacrament to be approached with awe, but I seem to be mistaken.

We are not alone in feeling that we kept our own children quiet, sometimes to the detriment of our own worship, and now that we are older, we feel we are entitled to the same consideration. There is the Sunday school and the crèche and really no need for it.

I appreciate that you fall between the pressures from both ends of the age spectrum and are in a difficult position. But is there really so much need to pander to the young?

The National Society and Church House Publishing have produced a book called *Leaves on the Tree,* about all-age learning and worship as a follow-up to *Children in the Way.* It deals in some detail with this particular problem and suggests practical ways of helping overcome it:

> The answer to the question, 'How do we expect children to behave in church?' usually depends on our answer to the question, *'Why* do we want children in church?' If we want them there because we believe they have as much right as we have to be there, equal members in their own right, then we shall want them to share our activities there as fully as possible. The main activity will be worship, so surely we shall want them to learn, week by week, the pattern of worship, to become familiar with the movements, the actions, the words.
>
> Whatever is being tried, it seems vital to keep in mind the needs of an all-age congregation. Having children present does not mean watering everything down, nor does it give a licence for toddler anarchy in and out of the pews... Worship should be a time, as a parishioner in a Yorkshire church said, when 'we are given permission to be ourselves, together'. We should expect from the youngest of us present a gradual recognition of all this; we should expect from the oldest of us present a gradual recognition that this may only be fully experienced when all ages worship together.[4]

7.24 This returns us to a recurring challenge to the churches. It is a two-pronged challenge: to commit human, financial and prayer resources to the task of bringing the message of God's love to children who do not know him; and to ensure that they are themselves equipped to offer all that is needed to those who respond to be welcomed and to grow within the Christian community.

8 Summary of Findings

(with questions for local churches)

8.1   The Working Party looked at the present situation facing children in society today. It recognised the enormous changes that have taken place since the Second World War, not least in the place that religion has within our culture.

8.2   It noted the serious decline in the churches' outreach to children since about 1955. In the 1950s the majority of our children were still encountering the gospel, half of them through Sunday schools. Today the situation has deteriorated, so that only about 14 per cent of our children encounter a church community.

How many children in your area have connections with local churches?

What percentage is that of the child population?

8.3   The churches tried, with some notable successes, to respond to the changing situation. New teaching materials reflected changes in teaching styles in schools. Again with some conspicuous successes, family worship, with more informal liturgical patterns and greater involvement, became part of parish life. Churches moved their Sunday schools from afternoon to morning; some moved them to another day of the week. Parishes tightened up their baptism policies to give opportunities for parents and godparents to have some learning experience of the Christian faith.

How does your church seek to involve children?

What is the parish Baptism policy?

8.4   These efforts however reached only those children whose parents were prepared to be involved themselves. Increasingly children were being marginalised from the Church.

8.5 The Working Party looked at the influences on youngsters today. It recognised that the vacuum left by the lessening of the Church's influence had been filled by other forces and messages. Some of these were good, many were not. It is certainly a fallacy to imagine that today's world is ideologically or morally neutral. It was also noted that childhood is being squeezed out, as children are pressured to share adult values and concepts.

What do you consider to be the major influences on the lives of children in your area today?

8.6 Changes in family life were noted. Higher standards of living are being financed by great debt. There are more families where both parents are financially employed, and this affects the time that the family can spend together. Increasingly many children are being brought up by one parent, whilst others are living with one natural and one step-parent.

What patterns of family life are to be found in your area?

What is the pattern of family life experienced by members of other faith communities in your area?

8.7 Today there is a marked increase in the number and range of out-of-school activities for children. Alongside this is an ever-increasing danger in the 'outside world', which leads to many children being transported to and from safe activities. Other children are left to fend for themselves in a world full of powerful temptations and dangers.

How do local children in your area spend their free time?

8.8 The power of television cannot be underestimated. It opens children to 'the ambiguous world of adult values and activities'. On the one hand, it can widen children's horizons, increase their knowledge, understanding and appreciation of the world and encourage compassion and generosity. But on the other hand, it can inhibit natural creativity, give a distorted view of reality, and introduce children to sex, violence and evil before they are emotionally able to cope with them.

What TV programmes do children watch?

How do you think those programmes affect them?

8.9 Commercial firms can exercise power and influence as they see children as targets for their marketing strategies. It is often children who decide what brand or product a parent should buy. Even toys play their part, encouraging children to build up collections, or enter a fantasy world where all is glamour and success.

8.10   Today's heroes are also used as part of a commercial and moral assault on our children. They are not simply idols, they are promoters of fashions, of activities, of attitudes.

Who are today's heroes for children?

What sort of life style do they present?

8.11   Into this scenario the Working Party began to identify some signposts for the Church's own involvement.

AN EVANGELISTIC IMPERATIVE

8.12   Evangelism among children is not an option for Christians, but should lie at the heart of our life and witness.

8.13   There is a *moral* imperative here. If, for whatever reason, we choose to leave the evangelism of children until they are older, then the battle may already be lost. The hearts and minds of our children are being forcefully moulded early in life.

8.14   There is a *spiritual* imperative. The kingdom of God belongs to children – all children – because they are who they are. God is for them. Thus they need to be helped to see that there is a God to whose kingdom they belong.

8.15   There is an *ecclesiastical* imperative. *Children in the Way* underlines that if the children are outside the Church, then those who are 'inside' are themselves impoverished. We need them as much as they need us.

How important is evangelism work among children in the life of your church?

What priority are you prepared to give it?

WHERE ARE THE CHILDREN WHO DO NOT COME TO CHURCH?

8.16   The answers need to be identified carefully, and the church must assess in the light of its resources and abilities where and when evangelistic activity will be staged.

8.17   Almost all children belong to a family. The report highlights some problems as well as opportunities here. The fifth commandment challenges us to take seriously the concerns of parents and the family. How can the Church be faithful to the divine imperative to evangelise, and yet honour the child's family who may be non-believers or adherents of another faith? How can we harness a general parental willingness to support anyone who is doing something good for their children?

Given your answers to 8.6, how does this affect any strategy you might have for work with children?

Are there children of other faiths in the parish? If so, what ought your approach to be to them?

8.18 Nearly all children go to school and spend much of their most active time there. The Church has a long and honourable history of involvement in schools. Education, including Religious Education, is undergoing many changes which reflect changes in society. Much teaching is experientially based. There are growing numbers of children of other faiths and cultures, whose views need to be respected. Yet there is also a demand for schools to be answerable to society (and especially to parents), to give value for money, and to show that standards are improving. It is in this complex, specialised and changing world that the Church still has the freedom to work. But she needs to be vigilant, ensuring that her activities, be they individual or corporate, are both educationally motivated and pastorally sensitive.

To which schools do local children go?

What relationships exist between Church and schools?

8.19 Whilst children spend much time in school and at home, they are also involved in activities outside. For some there are organised activities. For others, however, there are more dangerous attractions on street corners, in amusement arcades or shopping centres.

What do local children do out of school time?

WHO IS TO DO THE EVANGELISING?

8.20 Evangelism is the task of the whole Church. The Working Party did, however, identify a number of specific areas where we need to put some emphasis:

Clergy need to be trained both before and after ordination to develop skills of communicating with children individually and in groups. They need to be helped to relate to their local schools.

How can your clergy's ministry among children be supported and helped?

Christian parents need to be helped to contribute to the development and welfare not only of their own children but of others in the neighbourhood. They should be involved in the life and work of their children's schools.

What support is given to Christian parents?

Does your work with church-going children involve their parents?

Christians should be encouraged to give of their time and expertise in the service of children: to serve as governors of schools; to help run a club or organisation; to help in school or out-of-school activities.

Which members of your church are involved in work with children?

Who else might be encouraged to become involved?

Christians should be encouraged, and should encourage others, to train as teachers.

Which members of your congregation are teachers?

Can you identify any people whom you might encourage to become teachers?

Christians should support the work being done by Christian organisations: the Mothers' Union, Scripture Union, the Church Pastoral Aid Society, the missionary societies, uniformed organisations and many others. They should also use diocesan resources that are available, especially the work of children's advisers.

Do you know about any national organisations working with your children in your area?

Do you know what resources they can provide?

Do you know what resources your diocese can offer?

We need to recognise that denominational divisions are an irrelevance to children. We need to pool our resources and to work together with other Christians.

What are other churches doing in their work with children?

Do churches get together to share their work?

8.21 We recognised that many people are already working hard to build up our children, even though they may not work under the Churches' banner. Christians should be prepared to be involved in and to support such work – e.g. pre-school playgroups, nurseries, uniformed organisations such as the Scouting movement.

What other organisations are there for your children?

Are any members of your congregation involved?

How do you show that you care about and support this work?

8.22 Other partners in this enterprise are the children who already belong to our churches. With help and support they can be most effective evangelists with their peers.

How do you encourage children to bring their friends?

8.23 The church congregation itself can do much to help. It should affirm and support teachers and all who work with children by prayer, encouragement and resources.

Do you pray regularly as a congregation for teachers, leaders and others working with children?

Do you pray for them, or for their schools and organisations by name?

What resources do you as a congregation make available to them?

TIME AND PLACE ARE IMPORTANT

8.24 Research has shown that for many children Sundays are not the days when they are free to attend Church-run activities. Sunday is often the family day, and increasingly other temptations are apparent – football, outings, etc. The stories told in the previous chapter show how an imaginative choice of time and a suitable venue can play a significant part in the success or failure of an enterprise. Sunday schools emerged from the social situation of their day. What is suitable for the social situation in which you find yourself?

Is Sunday still a 'free day' in your area, when church-organised activities can hope to find significant response?

What other times can be identified when local children can be expected to be free?

Do your present events happen in suitable premises?

THE STYLE OF EVANGELISM IS IMPORTANT

8.25   Children seemed to gather around Jesus because he was an attractive character. He was then able to teach, to challenge and to encourage people to discover for themselves the truths of God's love. His attractiveness lay not in glitter and hype, but in his love for all whom he met and in his willingness to listen. He created a space in which they could find God for themselves.

8.26   What we have to offer must be similarly attractive.

Our Church, worship and people should have a strategy for helping people new to the faith to be introduced sensitively to the life of the Church.

What is your church's strategy?

Is it working?

We need a welcoming, well thought out and sensitive baptism policy with appropriate after-care not only for those who have been baptised, but for all children and their families.

Does your parish baptism policy need reviewing?

We need to be part of the Church's wider outreach, caring, for example, for mothers with young children.

We need to welcome into our homes children and families who live around us.

We need to see the evangelisation of children and their families as part of our own spiritual pilgrimage. It is not only what we can do for children, but what they can do for us.

What contribution do you think children make to the life of your church – and to you as individuals?

8.27   How we evangelise will need to be appropriate to the child. The insights of Faith Development understanding underline that both the approach we make to children, and the response we expect, must be appropriate to them.

8.28   How we evangelise will need to be appropriate to the particular area in which we minister. Communities, clubs and groups should reflect the needs of local children.

THE METHOD OF EVANGELISM MUST BE APPROPRIATE

8.29   Somewhere, somehow, the Christian story needs to be told. We need to be with the children where they are. We will attempt to show them by what we do and are that we care for them and for their needs. But the story needs to be told and learned, and children need to be encouraged to respond. Suitable people and suitable material need to be identified.

Whose task is it to tell the Christian story to children?

What resources do you/will you make available for this work?

Have you used the advice and resources available through your diocesan children's adviser?

8.30   Churches will also want to discover how the link can be made between evangelistic work in the home, in school and in the community on the one hand, and with the worshipping community on the other. They will have to ensure that what the children experience when they come into the worshipping community is a fair reflection of what they have experienced of Christian care and teaching outside.

What are your strategies for linking children in clubs and groups with the worshipping community?

Is your church welcoming to children and young families?

How can you improve matters?

TOGETHER INTO THE FUTURE

8.31   The Working Party believes that the Church must take the challenges of the Decade of Evangelism seriously. It is a God-given opportunity. We affirm that it must begin (but not end) with our work with children:

Individually we lack direction,
but, as a family, we have protection,
a balance that prevents us going wrong
too often and, if sometimes, not for long!
And no one needs to feel that he or she
has to take sole responsibility:
we're *all* involved – we each need one another;
mother needs child and child depends on mother,
the same is true for father, sister, brother.
So, each supplying what the others lack,
together we can trace the narrow track
that leads from childhood to maturity,
from earth to heaven – and what we're meant to be.

(Nigel Forde, *Children in the Way* video.)

Recommendations

1   **The Standing Committee of the General Synod** should report back to the Synod within 12 months on what arrangements have been made to ensure that the implications of this report have been followed through nationally within the Church of England and in partnership with other Churches.

2   **The Boards of Education and Mission** should approach *Churches Together in England* with a view to sponsoring a conference of those responsible in the Churches and voluntary agencies for the work of evangelism among children.

3   **Every Diocese** should identify a person to be responsible for encouraging and resourcing evangelism among children.

4   **Every Parish** should:

   • assess its present work in the light of this report, and take steps to ensure that the work has a high priority in its planning and resourcing;

   • encourage local Christians to support the work of Christian witness and the promotion of the spiritual development of pupils in schools by teachers, governors, parents and others;

   • examine the demands it is making upon and the support it is giving to Christian parents including support for the Mothers' Union and other similar agencies.

5   **Every Christian** should seek ways of witnessing to his or her faith among families and children.

6   **Everyone** concerned with children should ask what sort of Church and society they would like to see in 30 years time – and what needs to be done *now* in order to enable that vision to be realised.

Notes

INTRODUCTION

1. *Children in the Way: New Directions for the Church's Children* (NS/CHP, 1988).

CHAPTER 1

1. A sample of 2000 listeners to the BBC Daily Service.

2. Geoffrey Gorer, *Exploring English Character* (Cresset Press, 1955). He found parental support for Sunday schools to be significantly higher in Free Church circles than in Anglican.

3. Cited in *Growing Churches* (1957), a report on Church work among children in the context of English day school practice.

4. Peter Berger, *The Sacred Canopy* (Doubleday, 1969), p. 145.

5. Cited in *LandMARC* (1987).

6. Philip Cliff, *The Rise and Development of the Sunday School Movement in England, 1780-1980* (NCEC, 1986), p. 322.

CHAPTER 2

1. David Martin, *A Sociology of English Religion* (SCM, 1967).

2. Robert Towler, 'Conventional religion and common religion in Great Britain'. Paper 11 of the research project *Conventional Religion and Common Religion in Leeds* (Leeds University Sociology Department), pp. 11, 12.

3. Nicholas Abercrombie et al., 'Superstition and religion' in *A Sociological Yearbook of Religion in Britain*, (SCM) vol. iii.

4. Clifford Longley, Hockerill Educational Foundation Lecture (1988).

CHAPTER 3

1.   Norman Fowler, 'Labour force outlook to the year 2000', *Employment Gazette,* April 1989.

2.   See Lesslie Newbigin, *The Gospel in a Pluralist Society* (SPCK, 1989), p. 57. See also his comments on differing approaches to learning used in science and in religion, pp. 41, 43.

3.   'Family Matters', BBC1, 18 March 1991.

4.   Sir Robin Day, *Grand Inquisitor* (Pan, 1989), p. 329.

5.   *The Observer,* 24 May 1987.

6.   Ron Goulart, *The Assault on Childhood* (Victor Gollancz, 1970).

7.   *Children in the Way,* 1.4, p. 5.

8.   David Porter, *Children at Play* (Kingsway, 1989).

9.   Maggie Brown, *The Independent,* October 1990.

10. Jill Tweedie, *The Guardian,* 30 November 1981. Cited in *Children at Play,* p. 145.

11. David Porter, *Children at Risk* (Kingsway, 1986).

CHAPTER 4

1.   Hans-Reudi Weber, *Jesus and the Children* (NCEC, 1979), p. 9.

2.   William Barclay, *Matthew, Daily Study Bible* (St Andrew's Press, 1975), vol. ii, p. 212.

3.   Ibid., p. 11.

4.   Jürgen Moltmann, *The Way of Jesus Christ* (SCM, 1990), pp. 100, 101.

5.   Irenaeus, *Adversus Hacreses,* II. xxii. 4.

6.   Rebecca Manley Pippert, *Out of the Saltshaker: Evangelism as a Way of Life* (IVP, 1980), p. 16.

7.   *The Measure of Mission* (CHP, 1987).

8.   William Abraham, *The Logic of Evangelism* (Hodder & Stoughton, 1989).

9.   *The Measure of Mission*, p. 38.

10.   *The Logic of Evangelism*, p. 95.

11.   *Towards a Theology for Inter-Faith Dialogue* (CHP, 1988), p. 35.

CHAPTER 5

1.   *The Measure of Mission*, p. 38.

2.   For a further discussion of Fowler's theories, see *How Faith Grows: Faith Development and Christian Education* (NS/CHP, 1991).

3.   *Towards the Conversion of England* (1945), p. 89.

4.   John Stott, *Christian Mission in the Modern World* (Kingsway, 1975), p. 38.

5.   John Westerhoff, *Will our Children have Faith?* (Seabury Press, 1976), p. 39.

6.   Francis Bridger, *Children Finding Faith* (Scripture Union, 1988), pp. 120, 121.

CHAPTER 6

1.   Terence Copley, *Worship, Worries and Winners* (NS/CHP, 1989).

2.   *A Future in Partnership* (National Society, 1984), p. 71, cited in Geoffrey Duncan, *The Church School* (National Society, 1990), p. 5.

3.   George Oliver, *Religion in Schools: The Way Forward after the 1988 Education Act* (Christians in Education, 1988).

4.   See *School Worship* (National Society, revised edition 1991); Terence Copley, *Worship, Worries and Winners* (NS/CHP, 1989); Janet King, *Leading Worship in Schools* (Monarch, 1990); and *Collective Worship in County Schools* (Free Church Federal Council, 1990).

5.   *Faith in the Countryside* (Churchman Publishing, 1990), 10.40, p. 217.

6.   See *The Church School*, *The Curriculum: A Christian View*, *Governing Church Schools* and other booklets published by The National Society. Other resources for governors are available from the Department of Education and Science, diocesan boards of education and the National Association of Governors and Managers.

7.   *The Fourth R: The Durham Report on Religious Education* (NS/SPCK, 1970), pp. 103, 104.

CHAPTER 7

1.   *Faith in the Countryside*, p. 227.

2.   *Children in the Way*, 2.4, p. 15.

3.   *Faith in the Countryside*, p. 220.

4.   *Leaves on the Tree* (NS/CHP, 1990), pp. 17-19.

Do small churches hold a future for children and young people?

Leslie J. Francis and David W. Lankshear

SUMMARY

Seven thousand, one hundred and twenty-nine churches provided detailed information about their contact with children, young people and adults on a typical Sunday. Careful analysis of this information suggests that small churches which contact fewer than 26 adults experience special difficulty in maintaining an effective ministry among children and young people. The seriousness of this finding is assessed against the observation that two out of every five (41 per cent) Anglican churches have contact on a normal Sunday with fewer than 26 adults.

INTRODUCTION

According to the latest statistics published by the Statistical Unit of the Central Board of Finance,[1] about 1,161,300 people attend Church of England services on a normal Sunday, representing around 2.4 per cent of the total population. According to the official year book,[2] the 43 dioceses of the Provinces of Canterbury and York, excluding Europe, contain 16,704 churches. As a simple average this suggests a ratio of 69.5 worshippers for each church building, but simple averages can be grossly misleading.

While the statistics published by the Central Board of Finance do not permit a closer inspection of the Church of England's contact with children and young people, this lacuna has been partially filled by the survey undertaken to inform the General Synod report *Children in the Way*.[3] According to this source, the Church of England has contact with about 393,000 children and young people under the age of fourteen,

94

representing around 1.8 per cent of the total under two year olds, 3.2 per cent of two to five year olds, 6.8 per cent of six to nine year olds and 6.0 per cent of ten to thirteen year olds. As a simple average this suggests a ratio of 23.5 under fourteen year olds for each church building, but once again simple averages can be grossly misleading.

At the time of the 1944 Education Act,[4] much of the Church of England was confident that it could safely share the Christian education of the young with the whole of the state maintained system of schools. During the early 1970s, however, changes in educational theory,[5] in the understanding of the place of worship within the state maintained school[6] and in the definition of religious education[7] began to caution the churches' confidence in this arrangement. By 1976 the British Council of Churches' report, *The Child in the Church,*[8] was arguing strongly that the local congregation should accept responsibility for the Christian nurture of its young and find a warm place for the child at the heart of the worshipping community. In 1988 the Church of England's report, *Children in the Way,*[9] reinforced this view and offered the vision of all-age worship and all-age events for participating adults and children as fellow pilgrims, fellow learners and fellow teachers in the Christian way.

For this vision of the churches' responsibility for the Christian nurture of the young to be realised, each local congregation must be able and willing to accept and respond to the challenge to engage in effective ministry among children and young people within the context of all-age worship and all-age events. Moreover, if the local congregation fails to realise this vision and if at the same time the state maintained system of schools cannot be relied upon to undertake the churches' task on their behalf, both the Christian nurture of children and young people already 'in the way' and the Christian evangelisation of children and young people 'on the fringe' are likely to be seriously neglected. Not only are young lives at stake, but aspects of the churches' future are at stake as well. For example, in his study of the rural Anglican church, Francis[10] draws attention to small ageing congregations and raises a pertinent question regarding the future of these churches if their membership is not renewed by children and young people. Similarly, in their study of the rural Methodist church, Clarke and Anderson[11] document the gradual and persistent closure of chapels as ageing worshippers and trustees die and are not replaced by a younger generation.

RESEARCH QUESTION

Anecdotes about small churches and their ministry among children and young people may vary greatly. One person may tell of a small ageing congregation without a child in sight,[12] while another may describe a small church undertaking imaginative and successful work among children and young people.[13] Surely the same differences also appear in large churches, with some giving greater emphasis and showing greater success with work among children and young people than others. So what is the truth of the matter? Do smaller churches have greater difficulty in working among the young than larger churches, or not?

In order to address this question from an empirical research perspective, this paper re-analyses the data collected in the course of the survey undertaken to inform the report *Children in the Way*.[14] In this survey a detailed schedule was sent to every Anglican church or worship centre throughout 24 dioceses and one additional archdeaconry. At the time of the present analysis complete replies had been received from 7,129 places of worship, representing a response rate of 72 per cent.

Among other questions, the schedule asked each place of worship to log its total contact with people throughout two Sundays, including attendances at church services, Sunday schools, youth groups, parish discussion groups and all other activities. On the basis of this information it is possible to analyse the ratio between the number of adults and the number of children and young people contacted by churches of different sizes.

The assumption of this analysis is that, while it is totally reasonable to expect small churches to have contact with fewer children and young people than larger churches, it may also be reasonable to expect them, overall, to have contact with a similar ratio of children and young people in relationship to the number of adults contacted, if congregational life is to be renewed and maintained. The assumption is particularly pertinent in rural areas, where it is increasingly emphasised that each local congregation should reflect the total ministry of the church and be equipped to represent the fullness of the church of Christ in that place.[15] Moreover, while the significance of demographic changes needs to be taken into account, it is not yet true that children and young people have ceased to inhabit the countryside.[16]

RESEARCH FINDINGS

As the very minimum test of adequate involvement of children and young people, this paper proposes a ratio of one young person under the age of nineteen years for every *four* adults over the age of twenty-one years. The data demonstrate that the most effective churches on this criterion are those which have contact with over 75 adults on a normal Sunday. Nearly four-fifths (78 per cent) of the churches in this category have contact with at least one person under the age of nineteen years for every four adults over the age of twenty-one years. The proportion of churches which satisfy this criterion decreases significantly as the total number of adults contacted on a normal Sunday decreases. Thus, the criterion is met by a little over two-thirds (71 per cent) of the churches which contact between 51 and 75 adults, by a little under two-thirds (64 per cent) of the churches which contact between 26 and 50 adults and by only one-third (34 per cent) of the churches which contact fewer than 26 adults on a normal Sunday.

As a slightly tougher test of adequate involvement with children and young people, this paper proposes a ratio of one young person under the age of nineteen for every *three* adults over the age of twenty-one years. Once again, the data demonstrate a fairly consistent pattern for churches which have contact with over 75 adults on a normal Sunday. Nearly two-thirds (63 per cent) of the churches in this category have contact with at least one person under the age of nineteen years for every three adults over the age of twenty-one years. This criterion is also met by 56 per cent of the churches which contact between 51 and 75 adults, by 53 per cent of the churches which contact between 26 and 50 adults and by a little over one-quarter (28 per cent) of the churches which contact fewer than 26 adults on a normal Sunday.

What these statistics demonstrate is that, generally speaking, small churches which have contact with fewer than 26 adults experience especial difficulty in maintaining an effective ministry among children and young people. What these statistics do not demonstrate is that small churches must inevitably experience this difficulty. This point is reinforced by exploring the proportion of churches within different sizes which displayed peculiar excellence among children and young people.

As a test of excellence in involvement with children and young people, this paper proposes a ratio greater than one young person under the age of nineteen years for every adult over the age of twenty-one years. In accordance with this criterion, one in seventeen (6 per cent) of the churches which have contact with more than 75 adults on a normal Sunday has contact with a greater number of young people under the age of nineteen years than with adults over the age of twenty-one years. This criterion is also met by 6 per cent of churches which contact between 51 and 75 adults, by 7 per cent of the churches which contact between 26 and 50 adults and by 8 per cent of the churches which contact fewer than 26 adults. In other words, small churches which have contact with fewer than 26 adults are just as likely to pass this test of excellence in involvement with children and young people as larger churches.

The challenge focused by these statistics is to enable more small churches to recognise that it is truly possible for them to engage in effective ministry with children and young people and to develop all-age events and all-age worship. This is no small challenge, since the data also demonstrate that two out of every five (41 per cent) Anglican churches have contact on a normal Sunday with fewer than 26 adults, while nearly one more in every five (17 per cent) has contact with between 26 and 50 adults.

DISCUSSION

There is a number of reasons why small churches may find it particularly difficult to maintain effective contact with children and young people. Small churches may feel that they lack the necessary skills and appropriate qualities in lay leadership to accept responsibility for specialist work among the young. Small churches often need to share their clergy with other small churches and consequently the full-time stipendiary leader may feel unable to resource those areas of church life not adequately covered by indigenous lay ministry. Small churches often maintain an irregular pattern of Sunday services which may lack the continuity and accessibility attractive to children and young people. Small churches may find it difficult to orchestrate and to maintain high standards of liturgical presentation, music and teaching, consistent with the expectations of young people moulded by the professionalism of the media. Small churches often lack ancillary plant and consequently may be inhibited from offering specialist facilities for children and young people. Small churches may experience special difficulty in identifying appropriate curriculum and resources for fostering work among children and young people when there may be only one child within a given age category.

Young people themselves may feel particularly exposed and self-conscious worshipping in a small congregation. It is precisely these problems which all-age events described in publications like *Making Contact*,[17] *Springboard to Worship*[18] and *Signposts on the Way*[19] are designed to overcome. The General Synod report *Children in the Way* will have done a great service to small churches if it succeeds not only in putting children on their agenda, but also in encouraging them to experiment with all-age events and all-age worship.

NOTES

1. *Church Statistics: some facts and figures about the Church of England* (Central Board of Finance of the Church of England, 1989).

2. *The Church of England Year Book* (CHP, 1988).

3. L. J. Francis and D. W. Lankshear, 'The survey', in *Children in the Way* (NS/CHP, 1988), pp. 79-89.

4. H. C. Dent, *The Education Act 1944: provisions, possibilities and some problems* (University of London Press, 1947).

5. P. H. Hirst, 'Christian education: a contradiction in terms?' *Learning for Living*, 4 (2), 1972, pp. 6-11.

6. J. M. Hull, *School Worship: an obituary* (SCM, 1975).

7. Schools Council, *Religious Education in Secondary Schools* (Evans Brothers and Methuen Educational, 1971).

8. British Council of Churches, *The Child in the Church* (British Council of Churches, 1976).

9. *Children in the Way* (NS/CHP, 1988).

10. L. J. Francis, *Rural Anglicanism: a future for young Christians?* (Collins Liturgical Publications, 1985).

11. J. N. Clarke and C. L. Anderson, *Methodism in the Countryside: Horncastle circuit 1786-1986* (Clarke and Anderson, 1986).

12. See note 10 above.

13. A. Bowden, 'St Matthew's Church, Coates, Gloucestershire', in J. Richardson (ed.), *Ten Rural Churches* (MARC, 1988), pp. 15-34.

14. See note 9 above.

15. A. Russell, *The Country Parish* (SPCK, 1986).

16. M. Wilson (ed.), *The Rural Church: towards 2000* (Rural Theology Association, 1989).

17. L. J. Francis (ed.), *Making Contact* (Collins Liturgical Publications, 1986).

18. S. Sayers, *Springboard to Worship* (Kevin Mayhew Ltd, 1989).

19. M. Allen, A. Faulkner, N. Futers, S. Pearce and P. Privett, *Signposts on the Way* (Derby Church House, 1989).

Special services and events

David W. Lankshear, Marjorie Carnelley and Leslie J. Francis

SUMMARY

This brief survey draws attention to the variety of services and activities which churches have found to be effective in attracting greater than usual participation by children and young people. It would seem that the implications of this include:

(a)   the requirement that we use these occasions to present the Christian gospel to these children as effectively as possible;

(b)   the suggestion that churches which have not experimented with the range of activities listed should be challenged to review their position, in order to develop their ministry to this age group.

SOURCE OF INFORMATION

The project 'Children, Young People and the Church' was established in 1985 to examine the place of children and young people within the Church of England. A questionnaire was distributed during 1986 and 1987 to every Anglican place of worship in the following 24 dioceses: Bath and Wells, Birmingham, Blackburn, Bristol, Carlisle, Chelmsford, Chester, Chichester, Derby, Durham, Ely, Gloucester, Hereford, Lichfield, London, Oxford, Peterborough, St Albans, Salisbury, Sheffield, Southwell, Truro, Worcester, York and the archdeaconry of the Isle of Wight. In all, 7129 questionnaires have been returned, making a response rate of 71.9 per cent. This figure represents approximately two-fifths of all the Anglican churches in England. Comparison with key information provided by the statistical unit of the Central Board of Finance encourages us to believe that these churches may be relied upon to represent a cross-section of the Church of England as a whole.

The first publication of information collected in this survey was in the report, *Children in the Way* (National Society and Church House Publishing, 1988). The work was funded by grants from the Central Board of Finance of the Church of England, the St Christopher's Trust, the All Saints' Educational Trust, the Hockerill Educational Foundation, The Foundation of St Matthias, The St Gabriel's Trust, The Sarum St Michael Educational Charity and the Culham Trustees. The Management Committee represents the Diocesan Children's Work Advisers, The General Synod Board of Education and the Culham College Institute.

Among the information sought from the churches was a question designed to enable them to identify those special events in the life of the church which attract larger than normal numbers of children and young people. This question was intended to allow a flexible response, so that as many different activities should be reported as possible.

This report has been prepared without the inclusion of this information in the main data base. This has been done because of the wide range of individual reports, and the differing approaches adopted by churches to this section of the questionnaire. It is hoped that it may now be possible to incorporate the information, on which this study has been written into the main data base, as soon as funding becomes available.

SPECIAL EVENTS

In Chapter 7 of the report *Children in the Way* attention was drawn to the fact that between 7.5 and 10 per cent of the child population were in regular contact with the Church of England through attendance at Sunday services and the various activities which the parishes organise or sponsor for this age group on a regular basis, like Sunday schools, church choirs and so on.

When the churches gave details of events not otherwise reported in the questionnaire which attracted larger than normal attendance and participation by children they included the special and irregular occasions. It is these events which children who are on the fringe of the Church are likely to attend. Of the 7129 churches responding 4582 or 64 per cent indicated that they had one or more activities during the year which fell into this category.

While it has not been possible to report the number of children who attend these activities because many churches were unable to specify this information, it is possible to report the range and types of activity which the churches held. All the percentages are of the total number of churches in the survey (7129).

TYPES OF SERVICE

The following types of service were identified by significant numbers of churches as attracting more children than the normal attendance:

	Percentage of churches
Family services	33%
School services	20%
Parade services	17%

There may be some overlap between the family and parade services, but as most of the school services were held during the week they would seem to be a distinct category. It should also be noted that these family or parade services are reported as 'special events' in addition to the number of churches which report family and parade services as part of their regular week-by-week pattern of worship in other parts of the questionnaire. These two figures are, as a result, a conservative estimate of the number of churches holding these types of service.

While in this preliminary analysis it has not been possible to distinguish between different types of schools, it is clear that these include County as well as Church schools. Among the County and private schools every possible type of school seems to be represented, including schools for the handicapped.

All three of these categories also have links to particular points in the Church's year, which are reported on below.

Other services which were reported included:

Youth	3%
Weekday services for the under 5s and their parents	3%
Songs of Praise	2%
Sunday School Festivals	1%

Although Baptism was reported by only 1 per cent it should be remembered that a number of churches reported that they had held baptism services on the Sundays covered by the survey.

Confirmations were hardly reported, presumably because they do not attract children and young people who are not already involved in the Church, or because the churches did not see confirmation as relevant to this question.

THE CHURCH'S YEAR

The Church of England has an annual pattern of festivals and holy days, some of which relate to its role as a national Church. The occasions when additional numbers of children are likely to be present are:

Christmas	14%
Mothering Sunday	9%
Harvest	9%
Christingle	8%
Easter	5%
Remembrance	5%

These figures should be increased slightly to take account of the 2 per cent of churches who reported that they had additional children in attendance at 'the major festivals', without specifying which particular festivals.

Very few of the 7129 churches reported extra children attending at:

Patronal	2.0%
Rogation	0.9%
Flower	0.6%
Palm Sunday	0.6%
Civic	0.5%
Ascension	0.3%
Whitsun/Pentecost	0.3%

A number of other services were mentioned by some churches, but none of these were mentioned by more than 1 per cent. These included:

Mission Services
Industry Sunday Services
Plough Sunday Services
Memorial Services
Guest Services
Pet Services
Carnival Services

Healing Services
All Saints' Services

If this implies that those children who are on the fringe of the Church are more likely to participate in a service at these times, it is interesting to reflect on how their perception of the Christian gospel may be developing as as result of such an experience.

NON-SERVICE ACTIVITIES

While most churches responded to the question about the occasions which attracted large numbers of children and young people by focusing on services or the times of the year, a number reported the other activities in which they were engaged. The most frequently mentioned were:

holiday clubs	7%
outings and pilgrimages	2%
drama and musical events	2%
parties, (including Harvest Supper)	1%
activities involving the handicapped	«1%

A number of churches (4%) noted that their activities attracted more children when there was an ecumenical dimension to their work.

DIFFERENCES BETWEEN DIOCESES

While this report has focused on the national statistics it should be noted that there are some variations between dioceses. In some places there are local traditions such as Well Dressing or Rose Queen Services which attract large numbers of children in that area. There are also some local variations in the relative numbers of churches reporting attendance of additional numbers of children at different festivals. Thus there are two dioceses where there are more mentions of Christingle services than Christmas services, and ten in which Remembrance Sunday is mentioned more often than Easter. There is also one diocese where a majority of the churches did not report any activity at which children are in attendance in greater numbers than on a normal Sunday. However, in the main, the pattern appears to be consistent, and any variation between rural and urban dioceses appears to be more subtle than the current level of analysis will identify.

Afterword

Jim White: *Lord, help this wishy-washy dad*
(Reprinted with permission from *The Independent,* 27 April 1991)

A couple of weeks ago on Channel 4's *thirtysomething,* Michael, Hope's husband, was re-evaluating his life. He was wrestling with a problem that may have looked small, but loomed large in his mind: his infant son's equipment. Michael took 50 minutes fighting with his conscience, his upbringing and his wife before engaging the services of a rabbi and his scalpel for a fee of $30. Now the child was fully equipped (well, almost fully) to become a Jew. It made me wonder what I, pragmatic, wishy-washy, middle-class and English, have to offer my children as their heritage. What will tie them to their past, give them a historical connection to England and their Englishness, in the way circumcision locked Michael's child into his place in the Jewish scheme of things?

Prince Charles will probably have shaken some money out of the government by the time they get to school to ensure there are enough books to learn about Shakespeare, Byron, Jane Austen and D. H. Lawrence. There, too, they will learn the names of trees and wild flowers and the rules of hockey and rugby and will grow to appreciate that playing the game is more important than winning (unless it's against Manchester City).

Away from school it will be their parents' responsibility to help them develop a love of Lancashire cricket, MG roadsters and the Rolling Stones, and to introduce them to such mysteries of English life as why bitter tastes better from a straight glass and why your horse is always the first to fall in the National.

But there is something else, something that schools no longer regard as their responsibility. It is something my parents gave me, but which I will have difficulty bequeathing to my offspring. When our daughter was born in a hospital in London's East End there were three other mothers in the same ward. One was a Bengali Muslim, another was from the

Hassidic community of Stamford Hill and the third a fundamentalist Christian from Nigeria. Within hours of the birth, each of their children was visited by a local spiritual leader, who initiated them into their respective religion by circumcision or blessing. We talked about having our daughter christened. Two years later she still isn't.

When I was a boy, my parents took me to Sunday school, then to church, then encouraged me to join the choir. For seven years I went to church twice on Sunday and often several times on Saturday (we were paid 35p to sing at weddings, 50p at funerals). At 15, I gave church up. My parents were sensible enough not to object so this could not be glorified as rebellion.

Almost two decades later it never fails to amaze how much I remember. Once a year attendance has not dulled my memory of the Eucharist, nor the hymns, nor the language of the Bible and the Book of Common Prayer. Friends who didn't go to church, but attended the same number of school assemblies, are lost during each other's wedding services and need recourse to the hymn book for everything but 'Jerusalem' and 'Bread of Heaven' (they even seem surprised that the real words don't centre on supporting Man. United for ever more).

Most people lack any knowledge of the language and ritual of the Church of England. Most only have three points of contact with church: baptism, marriage and funerals – the hatch, match and dispatch of clerical jokes.

This is not surprising, as the disintegration of a family church-going tradition is rapid indeed. The *English Church Census,* published by the research organisation MARC Europe in March 1991, revealed that the chances of moving from regular church-going grandparent to completely secular grandchild are now nearing 50 per cent. In other religions the collapse may be more speedy. Young offspring of immigrant Muslims in Britain (particularly women) who find the strict demands of the religion intolerable, throw it off in a traumatic rebellion. It doesn't take so much to break with Anglicanism. But it is not so easy to drift back as it is to drift away: only 4 per cent of the children of non-church-goers become regular attenders.

The survey did not find any direct empirical evidence to support it, but there are other statistical data which suggest that one growth area in the Church of England (minor compared to America where 45 per cent of the population formally worships every weekend) is in young families. Parents seem to be sending their children back to Sunday school. They explain they want their offspring to learn the Bible stories that state schools don't teach any more. In inner-city areas it is not unheard of for parents to attend on Sundays simply to ensure the vicar's support in having their children enrolled in the local Church of England school – seen as an oasis of educational sanity.

Indeed the package of Christian myths and stories (Christmas, Easter and points in between) is as essential a part of our children's heritage as *Winnie the Pooh, Just So, William* or *Adrian Mole*. But the difficulty is that these other favourite stories don't come encumbered with moral baggage. William, Pooh and Mole are not didactic yarns, and though each might contain a lesson, it is basic stuff: the Hubert Laneites get their comeuppance, Pooh's greed gets him stuck fast in Rabbit's burrow, Mole gets his girl despite the mountainous white-heads. They certainly aren't metaphors for a code of ethics.

Some Anglicans argue that you can't have one without the other: the good tunes, the good words, the good stories are meaningless unless taken with a big dose of faith. That is where the problem comes. How can we, the lapsed, the unfaithful, lock our children into their cultural heritage without a bigger dose of hypocrisy? If we want them to have a real choice doesn't that imply they have to experience church in order to make the rational decision to reject it? This moral conundrum has had a most worrying side-effect, incidentally. I have found myself empathising with the life-re-evaluating dilemma of a *thirtysomething* character.

This article is included here not because it is totally consistent with the report's findings and recommendations, but because of the valuable insights the author gives to a contemporary parental dilemma which is part of the background to this report.